Halford John Mackinder

University Extension

Past, present, and future

Halford John Mackinder

University Extension
Past, present, and future

ISBN/EAN: 9783337036263

Printed in Europe, USA, Canada, Australia, Japan

Cover: Foto ©ninafisch / pixelio.de

More available books at **www.hansebooks.com**

UNIVERSITY EXTENSION,

PAST, PRESENT, AND FUTURE.

BY

H. J. MACKINDER,

READER IN GEOGRAPHY IN THE UNIVERSITY OF OXFORD;
STAFF LECTURER TO THE OXFORD UNIVERSITY EXTENSION;

AND

M. E. SADLER,

STUDENT AND STEWARD OF CHRIST CHURCH;
SECRETARY TO THE OXFORD DELEGATES FOR UNIVERSITY EXTENSION.

---

*BEING THE THIRD EDITION, REVISED AND ENLARGED, OF
"UNIVERSITY EXTENSION: HAS IT A FUTURE?"*

CASSELL & COMPANY, Limited:
LONDON, PARIS & MELBOURNE.
1891.

PREFACE.

THE first and second editions of this little book were published in August, 1890, under the title of "University Extension: Has it a Future?" They dealt, primarily, with the position created by the statement of the Chancellor of the Exchequer made in the House of Commons on the 21st of July, 1890, that part of the money accruing from the new spirit duty would ultimately be applied to the promotion of intermediate, technical, and agricultural education. Their object was to show that, from its past history and its present condition, the educational system, commonly known as University Extension, was worthy of serious attention whenever the Legislature should come to enumerate the institutions to which County Councils might vote grants in aid. The year which has elapsed since the autumn of 1890 has witnessed greater changes in English education than any which have happened since the memorable year 1870. Whilst the Imperial Parliament has been busy with Free Education, almost every County Council in England and Wales has been taking steps to initiate its own scheme of commercial and technical instruction. County Council aid has been given to University Extension Centres far sooner than a year ago we had any reason to expect; but in England it is limited to the promotion of teaching in scientific and other subjects capable of technical application. Already the Universities of Oxford and Cambridge have arranged for the coming winter, in conjunction with nine County Councils, about two hundred courses of instruction in Elementary and Agricultural Science, and other County Councils have made similar arrangements with other Universities and Colleges. It is certain, however, that the State aid thus given to other than elementary education cannot long remain one-sided in its character. Measures affecting general, intermediate, and higher education, on the literary and historical as well as on the scientific side, must be looked for in the immediate future. The organisers, central and local, of the University Extension system have, therefore, now to face administrative problems and imminent changes larger and more difficult to handle than any which have hitherto engaged their attention.

Under such circumstances, it is most encouraging to have to note that the increased demands upon its resources have only made more evident the vitality of the movement. The stimulus given by the County Council grants, and by the discussion and effort necessary to obtain them, has affected every branch of the system, which now reaches 45,000 students in England alone. In revising this book we have found that almost every detail in our previous account of the present state of University Extension is already out of date.

In the present edition the order of the chapters has been altered. That on "the Past" has been corrected in several details, and has been supplemented by a short account of the sister-movement in America. That on "the Present" has been carefully revised and brought up to date, while that on "the Future" has been partly re-written, in view of the altered prospects and problems before us.

We have only to add that, though we are personally connected with University Extension, we do not express the opinions of our colleagues or of the Delegates under whom we serve, and that, though we are associated especially with one branch of the movement, we aim at speaking in the interests of the whole. On subjects which have come to be matters of controversy we strive to represent, with fairness, the views of all parties.

H. J. M.
M. E. S.

Oxford, October, 1891.

CONTENTS.

	PAGE
CHAPTER I.—THE PAST	1
,, II.—THE PRESENT	46
,, III.—THE FUTURE	98

LIST OF ILLUSTRATIONS.

	PAGE
SKETCH DESIGN FOR UNIVERSITY EXTENSION COLLEGE . . . . *Frontispiece*	
UNIVERSITY EXTENSION CENTRES, 1885–86 ,, ,, ,, 1890–91	44
DIAGRAM SHOWING AVERAGE ATTENDANCE AT COURSES OF LECTURES . . . . . DIAGRAM SHOWING RESULTS OF EXAMINATIONS	45
OXFORD CENTRES, 1890–91 . . CAMBRIDGE ,, ,, . .	92
DESIGN FOR LIBRARY, UNIVERSITY EXTENSION COLLEGE	122
PLAN FOR UNIVERSITY EXTENSION COLLEGE. .	124

UNIVERSITY EXTENSION,

Past, Present, and Future.

CHAPTER I.

UNIVERSITY EXTENSION : THE PAST.

THE phrase "University Extension" first became current in the discussions on University reform which were prevalent in Oxford during the years immediately preceding 1850. A great number of influential members of the University had become deeply impressed with the importance of extending the benefits of University education to classes of students who were then excluded from the University by its regulations and arrangements. So long ago as in November, 1845, an address was presented to the Hebdomadal Board of the University of Oxford, asking the Board to adopt measures for the admission of a poorer class to the University.[1] Among the signatures appended to that address were those of Lords Sandon, Carnarvon, Westminster, and Ashley, Mr. Gladstone, Sir Thomas Acland, Mr. Sidney Herbert, Mr. Samuel Wilberforce (afterwards Bishop of Oxford), Mr. Tait (the late Archbishop of Canterbury), and others of high distinction. The petitioners did not content themselves with

[1] Report of the Oxford University Commission, 1852, p. 35.

merely asking the University to adopt their suggestions, but offered to give pecuniary assistance to the scheme. They sought, in the words subsequently used by Dr. Pusey,[1] "to enable the University to extend its benefits to talented and well-conditioned young men, however born, provided they shall be prepared to benefit by its education." "I was much struck," added Dr. Pusey, who supported the general purpose of this proposal, "in looking over the *Biographia Britannica* for the history of our divines, to observe how many of them were the sons of tradesmen." He also sought to confirm the new scheme by an appeal to ancient precedent. "In olden times," he pointed out, "the monks of Durham used systematically to send talented boys to be educated at the University." "The University," said Professor Hussey,[2] "seems bound to do something to meet the wants of the increasing numbers of the population; and especially to make more opening for those for whom a great part of its advantages were always intended—the youth of promise who have not at present the means of obtaining University education for themselves; not because they are poor merely, as objects of pity, nor yet as a different order, to be distinguished by badges; but because they show talent, and industry, and willingness, and desire to improve themselves, and because they ought not to be shut out from advantages open to other persons, with whom they might perhaps compete successfully." The object

---

[1] Report and Evidence upon the recommendations of Her Majesty's Commissioners, presented to the Board of Heads of Houses and Proctors, Dec. 1, 1853. Oxford, 1853, p. 79.

[2] *Ibid.*, pp. 233, 234.

of this important movement was well summed up by Mr. Osborne Gordon,[1] of Christ Church, who said, "I look for the extension of the University to the poor."

There was, indeed, much in the condition of the University of Oxford which called for a change. The expenses of collegiate life, especially when compared with the common standard of that time, were great, while the subscription to the Thirty-nine Articles required at matriculation, and the subscription to the three Articles of the Thirty-sixth Canon on presentation for a degree, excluded one class of the community from University education. As to the propriety of making any alteration in the religious tests, there was, of course, grave difference of opinion, both in the University and outside it; but men of all parties seem to have felt the importance of facilitating the admission of a poorer class of students to the privileges of University life. The strength and prevalence of this feeling is proved by the evidence given before the Oxford University Commission of 1850. "I believe," said Mr. Arthur Clough,[2] in the considerations which he submitted to that Commission, "I believe in the possibility of a gradual, sure, and ultimately large extension of the old Universities." "The ideal of a national University," Mr. Mark Pattison[3] argued before the same body, "is that it should be co-extensive with the nation; it should be the common source of the whole of the higher (or secondary) instruction for the country." "The

---

[1] Report and evidence upon the recommendations of Her Majesty's Commissioners, p. 198.
[2] Oxford University Commission, 1853. Evidence, p. 213.
[3] *Ibid.*, Evidence, p. 44.

University," he continued, quoting from Gordon, "should strike its roots firmly into the subsoil of society, and draw from it new elements of life and sustenance of mental and moral power."

It appears that this widely-felt desire to extend the usefulness of the University had led to the proposal of several schemes, which, as was believed by their advocates, would, separately or conjointly, accomplish the design cherished by so many influential graduates. These "plans for University Extension" were accordingly summarised by the Commissioners, and an official stamp was thus given to an expression which had been found to conveniently designate the movement for the spread of University effort into new and wider fields of national life. Seven schemes of University Extension were mentioned by the Commissioners,[1] and four of these were discussed in detail. The plans were as follows:—

1. The establishment in the University of new Halls, as independent Societies or in connection with Colleges.
2. Permission to Undergraduates to lodge in private houses more generally than at present.
3. Permission to Students to become members of the University, and to be educated at Oxford under due superintendence, without subjecting them to the expenses incident to connection with a College or Hall.
4. Admission to Professorial Lectures of persons to whom the Professors should be authorised to grant certificates of attendance, without any further connection with the University.
5. The abolition of Religious Tests on matriculation and graduation.
6. The foundation of Theological Schools in Cathedral cities, and their affiliation to the University. The affiliation to the University of Lampeter College and of the Theological College at Birkenhead.
7. The provision of funds by the University for the

[1] Oxford University Commission, 1853. Report, pp. 35-56.

establishment of professorial chairs in Birmingham and Manchester; sufficient attendance at the lectures of these Professors to be accepted as qualifying for a degree.

The Commissioners did not consider that the examination of all these schemes fell within the scope of their enquiry. Indeed, the fifth proposal, involving the admission of Nonconformists to the University, implied a question which they were instructed not to entertain. On this head, therefore, they contented themselves with expressing their "conviction that the imposition of subscription in the manner in which it was (then) imposed in the University of Oxford, habituates the mind to give a careless assent to truths which it has never considered, and naturally leads to sophistry in the interpretation of solemn obligations."

The fourth proposal—namely, that for the admission to Professorial Lectures of persons who were not matriculated members of the University—was found to have been already anticipated by common practice.

The Commissioners approved of the first three plans for University Extension, and, as is well known, residence in lodgings outside the walls of his College has since become the almost invariable experience of every undergraduate during part of his academical career; while the body of non-collegiate students, residing in Oxford without being attached to any College or Hall, has become an important part of the University.

These schemes, however, were rather of a domestic nature. They have affected the internal life of the University, and have increased, for large numbers and many new classes of students, the convenience of its arrangements. But it is rather to the remaining proposals for the affiliation of local colleges and for the establishment of teaching in large towns that we turn for the origin of the movement, which is now specifically called University Extension. Oxford has now for a long time adopted the principle of affiliating to itself, on certain conditions, educational institutions outside the University,[1] while Cambridge has taken the further step of offering the advantages of affiliation to a number of towns which, while not possessing any collegiate buildings, are yet supporting a comprehensive and systematic scheme of education.

The First Proposal for University Extension Teaching, 1850.

The germ, however, of University Extension, as we now understand it, is to be found in the idea that it would be right and politic for the University to provide funds for the maintenance of Professors in Birmingham and Manchester.[2] This proposal was made by Mr. Sewell, Fellow and Senior Tutor of Exeter College, and afterwards Warden of Radley, in a letter addressed to the Vice-Chancellor of Oxford, in the year 1850, and entitled "Suggestions on University Extension."[3]

---

[1] *See* "Statutes of the University of Oxford." Ed. 1889, pp. 6-8.

[2] *See* p. 50.

[3] "Suggestions for the Extension of the University submitted to the Rev. the Vice-Chancellor by Wm. Sewell, B.D." Oxford, 1850. The idea may have been suggested to Mr. Sewell by the bequest, in 1846, by Mr. John Owens of £96,000 for the foundation of a college in Manchester. In announcing the bequest on Aug. 6, 1846, the *Manchester Guardian* stated that Mr. Owens had left this large sum " for the purpose of affording to youths of the age of fourteen years and upwards instruction in the branches of education taught at the English Universities, free from the religious tests, *which limit the extension of University Education.*" The Owens College was opened in 1851. Compare Thompson: "The Owens College: Its Foundation and Growth." Manchester, 1889.

"Though it may be impossible to bring the masses requiring education to the University," wrote Mr. Sewell, in words which have been re-echoed by many later advocates of University Extension, "may it not be possible to carry the University to them? Yes," he replies, "and at first, by way of experiment, professorships and lecturerships might be founded, say at Manchester and Birmingham, the great centres of manufacturing districts, and in the midst of the densest population. They would require little cost beyond the stipends of the Professors engaged. . . . By degrees the system might be extended through the whole country, and similar institutions might be planted in the principal towns in convenient districts, such as Norwich, Exeter, Leeds, Canterbury, Newcastle, &c. &c. Cambridge would, of course, take its due share of the work. . . . A plan of this kind would extend the benefits of University instruction to the utmost possible limits. It would reduce the expense to the lowest point. . . . Wherever its institutions were planted, the immediate residents would be provided with the opportunity of completing the education of their sons, without parting with them from under their own roof. . . . And, lastly, by originating such a comprehensive scheme, the Universities would become, as they ought to be, the great centres and springs of education throughout the country, and would command the sympathy and affection of the nation at large, without sacrificing or compromising any principle which they are bound to maintain."

It is interesting to conjecture what results might have followed from the early adoption of this idea.

The judgment, however, of the Commissioners was adverse to it. "If," they wrote, "the means of the University were unbounded, its superfluities might possibly be employed on the general purposes of education throughout the country; but such a scheme should not be entertained till it has been shown that there is no demand for men and for money in the University itself." It is to be regretted that the Commissioners did not realise the importance and suggestiveness of Mr. Sewell's proposal, and failed to perceive that hardly any more useful task was then imposed on the University than to co-operate with the friends of higher education, resident in the large towns, in the gradual provision of opportunities for such education in those great industrial centres. It is fortunate that, at a later time, both the old Universities have found it compatible with the proper care and encouragement of the studies within their own walls, to expend a portion of their revenues in stimulating the love of learning among those whom home ties or business duties absolutely prevent from undertaking any prolonged period of residence within the Universities themselves.

Such, then, was the first publication to the country of the idea of University Extension.[1] It is singular that among all the various schemes not one, even remotely, entertains the project of providing in the University the means of higher education for women. But, with this one exception, the proposals for University Extension put forward in Oxford at the time of the first Univer-

[1] For an account of mediæval anticipations of University Extension, see the *Quarterly Review* for April, 1891. Article: "University Extension in England."

sity Commission anticipated the various sides of the movement, which ever since has gone on steadily gaining ground. The great prominence given to the subject in the report of the University Commission, shows that it was particularly in Oxford that public opinion was first deeply moved by the necessity of adjusting the regulations and requirements of the University to the needs of large and deserving classes who had been excluded from it; but, five years after the publication of Mr. Sewell's pamphlet, an approving voice came from Cambridge. In 1855 Lord Arthur Hervey (now Bishop of Bath and Wells) published what he called "A Suggestion for Supplying the Literary, Scientific, and Mechanics' Institutes of Great Britain and Ireland with Lecturers from the Universities."[1] This little pamphlet of twenty pages is of extreme interest, and seems to have been overlooked in most previous accounts of the growth of University Extension. The writer remarks that "of all the features of the present day which indicate the growing desire of the industrious classes for intellectual improvement, none is more prominent than the multiplication of Mechanics' Institutes." "The Institutes," he continues, "arrange lectures for their members." But the educational value of these isolated lectures is uncertain, and their character "desultory and unconnected." It must often be a great disappointment to an intelligent hearer, in whom a desire to be acquainted with geology has been excited by a

---

"A Suggestion for Supplying the Literary, Scientific, and Mechanics' Institutes of Great Britain and Ireland with Lecturers from the Universities." By Lord Arthur Hervey, M.A., Cambridge. (Macmillan and Co. 1855.)

lecture on the subject, to find that the next lecture is on Scotch poetry and the one after on metaphysics, and that there is not another geological lecture in the whole course. " Thus the best lectures, not being followed up, come short of the good which they might otherwise do." But could not the Mechanics' Institutes get connected courses by competent lecturers? " Turn to the Universities," says the author. " It has been an obvious matter of consideration to them, as to the legislature, whether they cannot in any way enlarge and widen the circle of their direct action, and make themselves in a yet fuller sense the educators and enlighteners of the country. Nor could anything more conduce to their conciliating to themselves the affection and support of all classes in the land than the devising of some means by which all classes should derive direct instruction and pleasure from the fountain-head of the Universities themselves." Lord Arthur Hervey thus points out that there are the voluntary literary associations, on the one hand, seeking lecturers; while, on the other, the Universities, "the great depôts of learning and science," are able to provide lecturers for them. "And," he adds, "by a most happy coincidence, the wonderful invention of railroads has brought into easy communication with the Universities districts which were before remote and inaccessible."

The writer then passes on to the practical details of his scheme. "Four new Professors, who might be called *rural* or *circuit* Professors, are to be nominated by the University." As their subjects, he suggests Natural Philosophy, Geology, Astronomy, and Literature. " The courses in some places would consist of more, in some of less, than six lectures." But it is interesting to note that in this scheme for University Extension, published by a member of the University of Cambridge, the course of six lectures is taken as the normal unit of organisation. Each Professor is to give 120 lectures a year—*i.e.*, six lectures in each of 20 towns : between them the four Professors will thus visit 80 towns per annum. For every course of six lectures, each Institute might contribute, on an average, £20. "This would give an annual income of £1,600 to be divided among the four Professors, or £400 a year to each. If, in addition to this, fellowships could be attached to the Professorships, a handsome income would be provided. And, if the same system were adopted at Oxford, at the University of London, at Trinity College, Dublin, at the Scotch Universities, and eventually at Durham, we might look forward to having the whole of the United Kingdom brought within reach of the best instructors the country can afford."

One circumstance alone, however, was sufficient to cause any elaborate scheme for the extension of University teaching in large towns to be, at that time, regarded as premature. The University Extension system, as we now understand it, depends on our railway system. It would be impossible for it to work without our modern service of quick and frequent trains. Anyone who compares the Bradshaw of to-day with the Bradshaw of 1855 will see at once a sufficient reason why the idea of University Extension teaching did not strike root when Mr. Sewell's and Lord Arthur Hervey's proposals appeared. In his pamphlet on University

Extension,[1] Dr. Roberts, whose efforts during the last fifteen years have been widely useful in the diffusion of University teaching, points out that the University Extension movement of to-day is fulfilling one of the pious hopes of the founder of Clare College, who desired to see an increase in the number of students, "to the end that the precious pearl of knowledge, having been found by them, and made their own by study and instruction in the University, might not be hidden under a bushel, but be spread abroad beyond the University, and give light to them that walk in the dark paths of ignorance." Under changed conditions University Extension is thus realising some of the ideals of the past. But the present scheme is not so much to bring to the Universities the modern representatives of those great multitudes who in old days flocked to it. Its aim is rather to take some of the opportunities of University education to them, in the belief that, by adjusting their arrangements to the various needs of the different classes of the community, the Universities, without losing any part of their present dignity and usefulness, will more and more conform to the ideal of truly national institutions.

Sir Thomas Acland and the Beginning of the Local Examinations. Hardly had the University Commission of 1850 concluded its labours, than a step was taken by an association in London which had, indirectly, an important effect on the development of University Extension. The Society of Arts established in

---

[1] "The University Extension Scheme as the Basis of a System for National Higher Education," by R. D. Roberts, M.A., D.Sc. (Lond.) Aberystwyth, 1887. Compare also the same writer's "Eighteen Years of University Extension" (Cambridge, 1891), pp. 10, 11.

1854 a series of examinations for Mechanics' Institutes. In 1852 the Society had taken the lead in forming a union of Mechanics' Institutes, to which more than 300 of them became affiliated. Two years later the Society arranged to hold examinations for the members of these Institutes, and to offer certificates of competency to those who acquitted themselves in the examination with credit. These examinations, in which the present Bishop of London acted as one of the examiners, proved completely successful; and were designed specially with a view to stimulating the studies and testing the knowledge of adults.

But, important as the work was among adults, it was soon felt that there was an even greater need for similar examinations designed for boys at school. "The education of the middle classes," Dr. Temple wrote to the Master of Pembroke College, Oxford, in April, 1857, "suffers from the want of any definite aim to guide the work of the schoolmasters, and from the want of any trustworthy tests to distinguish between good and bad schools." Lord Ebrington, accordingly, had called attention in 1855 to the examination designed by the Society of Arts for the adult members of Mechanics' Institutes, and in conjunction with Mr. (now Sir Thomas) Acland and the Rev. J. L. Brereton, promulgated a scheme for the examination of middle-class schools in the west of England. The further development of the idea is described in a book subsequently published by Mr. Acland.[1] It appears from his account that the operations of

---

[1] "Some Account of the Origin and Objects of the New Oxford Examinations for the Title of Associate in Arts and Certificates for the Year 1858. By T. D. Acland." London, 1858.

the Bath and West of England Society for the Encouragement of Agriculture, Arts, Manufactures, and Commerce brought together a number of persons engaged in different occupations, but with a common object in view. Among these persons "a thirst for knowledge was excited and a consequent sense of the evils of neglected education awakened. Accordingly, a few persons of various shades of opinion, political and religious, having learned to act together and to trust each other, provided a small prize fund with a view to put to a practical test the value which the middle ranks might be disposed to attach to certificates of the progress of their children, if awarded by competent examiners."[1] This Committee, to which Mr. Acland acted as secretary, was formed at Exeter in the early part of 1857, and met with substantial encouragement from the Bath and West of England Society later in the same year. The machinery devised by Mr. Acland consisted of a Local Examination Committee of thoroughly representative persons resident in the locality, and of a Board of Examiners, among whom were Sir Stafford Northcote, Professor Max Müller, Mr. George Richmond, Mr. John Hullah, and Dr. (now Sir Henry) Acland. But the Local Committee, in order to give to their work as much of an official stamp as was possible under the circumstances, asked the Committee of Council on Education to allow two of Her Majesty's Inspectors of Schools to co-operate with the examiners locally appointed. The request was granted, and the Lord President instructed

[1] "Some Account of the Origin and Objects of the New Oxford Examinations for the Title of Associate in Arts and Certificates for the Year 1858. By T. D. Acland." London, 1858, pp. 96, 97.

the Rev. F. Temple (now Bishop of London) and Mr. J. Bowstead "to afford assistance in giving effect to the scheme of examination and prizes."

The examination, which took place in June, 1857, was regarded by Mr. Temple "as the first step towards the improvement of middle-class education,"[1] and similar examinations were organised in the counties of Staffordshire, Cheshire, Shropshire, Warwickshire, and in South Wales. Clearly there was beginning a general and spontaneous movement for the improvement of middle-class education, and "the intellectual life of the people was pushing forth vigorous shoots in various directions."[2]

The details of this local effort are historically interesting because they gave the stimulus to the next step in University Extension. Mr. Acland's original scheme was avowedly experimental. If it succeeded, it was his hope that it would be followed up by some recognised authority, his own desire being that the Universities should themselves organise and superintend similar local examinations in different parts of the country. He pointed out "that the religious exclusiveness of the Universities had been removed by Act of Parliament; . . . that, as regards secular knowledge, they were in a favourable position for combining much freedom with much exactness; . . . that, in the department of the Arts, they had great advantages in their libraries and collections; . . . and that many of their members possessed experience of the official work of public education going on in the country."[3] It was also pointed out

[1] *Ibid.*, p. 192, Mr. Temple's Report.
[2] *Ibid.*, p. 98. [3] *Ibid.*, p. 10.

that the many graduates of the Universities who occupied important posts in the large towns, and were connected with the administration of justice and the management of public institutions in country districts, formed a natural body of supporters for the new scheme, the success of which would depend on the cordial co-operation between the local committees and the central authorities in the Universities. The great position of the Universities would "be a strong security that no private crotchets or personal interests would be allowed to disturb the action of a great body of men for the mental cultivation of a free people."[1]

"A career of almost unbounded usefulness," wrote Mr. Acland in 1858, "seems open to the Universities if they will respond to the call of the nation for aid in supplying a better general education to the great body of their countrymen. Their fortunate position within reach of, but not within, the Metropolis, their traditional associations, their comparative independence of pecuniary interest, their connection with so many parishes and grammar-schools, all seem to point them out as eminently qualified to give a healthy and liberal tone to school education as a preparation for the busy occupations of agricultural and commercial life, no less than for literary and scientific pursuits."[2]

Such was the new proposal which was put before the Universities. They were asked to extend their usefulness by taking for the first time a definite part in the education of persons who had not been

---

[1] "Some Account of the Origin and Objects of the New Oxford Examinations for the Title of Associate in Arts," p. 11.
[2] *Ibid.*, pp. 98, 99.

matriculated. Memorials supporting the request poured in from different parts of the country. Interest was aroused first in Oxford, immediately afterwards in Cambridge; and with little delay the system of local examinations "of those who were not members of the University" was adopted by both the old Universities. "To borrow a happy illustration from the originator of the 'Oxford Extension Scheme,'" wrote Mr. Acland in 1858, "Oxford has opened a locomotive department, and the first line of rails was laid down by the West of England."

The new idea was now firmly established. The Universities had recognised their educational duty towards the country in a wider sense than ever before; and the promoters of the new scheme had devised and tested a system which combined local self-government with the advantages of central supervision and management. Local business was entrusted to the voluntary local committees; the educational policy of the movement was rightly reserved for the Universities themselves.

Such a sensible and practical arrangement was sure to develope. And, detail by detail, new branches were added to the work. Girls were examined as well as boys: more advanced students as well as children.

It soon, however, became apparent that the system was capable of a still wider extension. Teaching was required as well as examination. The generosity of wealthy citizens was, in many great towns, stimulating the work of higher education. All over the country there were signs of a freshly-quickened desire for knowledge and an eagerness to obtain it at the hands of the best teachers. The higher education of women was making rapid advances; and the "sharp struggle" which preceded the Education Act of 1870 had already begun.

<small>Professor Stuart and the Beginning of Local Lectures.</small>

The next step, therefore, was to make the machinery of the local examinations available for the purpose of local lectures. This great advance was due to the energy of Professor Stuart, who is deservedly regarded by all workers in the movement as the father of University Extension in its present form.

In 1867 he received an invitation from an association of ladies in the north of England to give some lectures to them.[1] The President of the Association was Mrs. Josephine Butler, the Secretary Miss A. J. Clough. He was asked to lecture on the art of teaching. He replied that he had not experience enough to lecture on that subject, but, "as a thing is often best described by showing a piece of it," he offered to give a course of eight lectures, in which he would endeavour to teach something. There was special point in this offer of a *course* of lectures: Professor Stuart had been "vexed with the insufficiency of the single-lecture system which prevailed in connection with Mechanics' Institutes and Literary Societies." He was convinced that, if teaching was to be systematic, it must be embodied in a course. Twenty

---

[1] "Inaugural Address of Professor Stuart at the Second Summer Meeting of University Extension Students in Oxford, July 30, 1889," p. 20. Compare also "Report of the First Meeting of the North of England Council for Promoting the Higher Education of Women." Manchester: Beresford and Havill (1868). Among the members of this Council were Professor Bryce, Dr. Fitch, Professor T. H. Green, and Mr. Henry Sidgwick.

years later Mr. Barnett remarked that University Extension must now aim at substituting for the casual course of lectures (history fortuitously following science, and literature political economy) the series of courses arranged in some more definite sequence. The first battle, however, of University Extension, when Professor Stuart took up the cudgels, was to substitute the course of lectures by the same teacher for a disconnected series of isolated addresses by separate lecturers. Nor was Professor Stuart alone in his contention. Professor Henry Morley, and others with him, had, after several years of effort, succeeded at last in getting the public to understand that it is much more interesting to follow one teacher through a subject than to listen to a succession of men, severally complaining that they have not time, in the limits of one lecture, seriously to attempt to teach it. Professor Stuart's courses were given in 1867 at Leeds, Liverpool, Manchester, and Sheffield. They were well attended, but the audiences were composed of women only. Thus, in its first beginnings, University Extension was set on foot by women. And ever since that time women have formed a large part of University Extension audiences. These first courses of Professor Stuart were, however, interesting, not only because they were practically the origin of University Extension teaching, but because they suggested two arrangements which are still important features in the system. These were the syllabus and the weekly exercises. The syllabus was devised as a lesson in note-taking: Professor Stuart says that he got the idea from Professor Ferrier of St. Andrews, "who used, in connection with some of his more difficult lectures, to dictate a series of heads which were found to be an immense assistance." The other feature, the weekly exercises, were hit upon as a compromise which would avoid the necessity of orally questioning the audience—a rather embarrassing experience, which the lecturer agreed with the majority of his students in wishing to avoid. The first course of lectures was followed by many others. Several other graduates were invited to lecture; but the arrangement was made in each case *ad hoc*, and a difficulty arose from the fact that the lecturers could be offered nothing approaching to permanent employment.

How then was the scheme to be systematised? Professor Stuart's first proposal was "to form a central committee permanently engaging lecturers at a salary, and sub-letting them, so to speak, to local associations." There was much to recommend this plan: even now there is much to be said in its favour. Had it been adopted, we should to-day have been working University Extension as an affair of business. It would have been "University Extension, Limited"; but there were two obstacles to its adoption. One fatal objection is, that no company, working merely on business methods, could command the same prestige in the educational world as a committee appointed by and representing the Universities. Such a company might conceivably have been freer to make experiments: it would almost certainly have been able to command larger resources of capital for the retention of experienced or promising lecturers. But it would not have enjoyed the same status. It would not have had at its back the same wealth of associations. Its work would not have appealed in the same way to the affectionate interest of the old University men, who, scattered as they are in positions of influence all over the country, form, as Sir Thomas Acland had seen years before, the natural supporters and local agents of such part of the work of the University as cannot be conducted in the University town itself. In the case, however, of Professor Stuart's proposal, when it was first broached, this objection, though doubtless realised, did not seem so serious as the merely temporary want of funds. This drawback would soon have been overcome, but at the time it was insuperable. " The whole proposal," said Professor Stuart, " was, I suppose, premature."

The movement, however, soon took a new departure. One of the junior managers at the Crewe Railway Works, Mr. Moorsom, wrote to Professor Stuart in 1867, urging him to come and give a lecture to the workmen there. The invitation was accepted. The subject of the lecture was "Meteors," and it received a gratuitous advertisement from a remarkable shower of meteors which fell on the night before. The lecture met with such acceptance that it led to the delivery of a course of lectures similar to those which had been given to women. The course at Crewe was followed by one to the members of the Equitable Pioneers' Society at Rochdale, an association of workingmen which bears an honoured name in the economic history of England. It was at Rochdale that Professor Stuart invented "the class," the period of conversational teaching, enlivened by brisk episodes of "heckling," which has ever since been an important feature in the University Extension System. The origin of the class was simple. The lectures were illustrated by diagrams. Professor Stuart wanted the diagrams which had illustrated one lecture to remain on the walls till his next appearance, as he proposed again to refer to them. The hall-keeper demurred, as, in the interval between the lectures, the society was going to meet in the same hall for the discussion of business. However, leave was at last obtained, and it transpired that members who attended the meeting were so attracted by the diagrams that they stayed behind to discuss them for a whole hour. They, had, indeed, asked the door-keeper to invite Professor Stuart to come to the lecture-room before the next lecture, in order that they might ask him some questions. He did so, and thus began the first University Extension "class."

Establishment of Girton and Newnham Colleges.

Two years later the position of the University Extension scheme was strengthened by the striking development of an independent, though related, branch of the movement for higher education. In 1869 Girton College was founded at Hitchin. Four years afterwards it was removed to Cambridge, where, in the meantime, Newnham College had been founded in 1871.

Official Recognition of Extension Teaching by the University of Cambridge.

The rapid growth, however, of the University Extension scheme itself soon brought heavier responsibility. It became clear that there must be some central organisation for the supply of competent lecturers from the University. In its system of Local Examinations, the University already supplied examiners. Why not lecturers too? It had the men, it had the machinery, it had the prestige. Accordingly, in November, 1871, Professor Stuart addressed a letter on the subject to the University of Cambridge.[1] He submitted to the University what was, in effect, the same proposal as that made to the University of Oxford by Mr. Sewell twenty years before. But, in the meantime, things had moved forward. The system of Local Examinations had been devised and found to work well. The times were ripe for the new idea. There was evidently a public demand for University teaching. Professor Stuart's own experience had proved the reality of that demand and the possibility of satisfying it. He did not merely fire off a casual suggestion into the air. He came forward with a practical scheme.

"The demand for education exists," he told the University. Would they supply it or not? "I believe," he wrote,[2] "that it is incumbent on us to supply it, and I believe that some such system, which will carry the benefits of the University through the country, is necessary in order to retain the University in that position with respect to the education of the country which it has hitherto held, and to continue in its hands that permeating influence which it is desirable that it should possess." It was now admitted on all hands that the Universities were not clusters of private establishments, but national institutions. Pressing this home, he argued that some such scheme as he advocated would be "a great step towards making the Universities truly national institutions, and be no less beneficial to them than to the country."

For, if the University is a national institution, it

---

[1] "A Letter on University Extension, Addressed to the Resident Members of the University of Cambridge, by James Stuart." Cambridge, 1874.

[2] "Letter on University Extension," quoted above.

should so accommodate its arrangements as to make some of them available for everybody. That was the drift of the new demand. "By permitting the residence of non-collegiate students," Professor Stuart wrote, "we have taken a great step towards rendering our Universities accessible to all classes." But one reform inevitably leads to the suggestion of another. "This expression 'all classes,'" he pointed out, "only includes those who can procure some years of continuous leisure, which is far harder to get than the requisite money. Among those classes whose circumstances debar them from residing at a University, there exists a widespread desire for higher education of a systematic kind."

Professor Stuart's proposals had at their back the force of the new educational movement. Long and bitter controversy had ended in the Elementary Education Act. A fresh interest had been awakened in the question. The public mind had been prepared for educational advance. The desire for higher education had been quickened. Far-seeing people perceived that, when the seeds of elementary education had been sown, a new generation would arise, with new ideals of life and new gifts of knowledge. Something must be done betimes for that generation, or the very education with which the State had decided to equip it would prove a national danger. Education must not end with the school.

But what was to be done? Would it be enough to offer them merely popular lectures? This, Professor Stuart said, would be like giving them a stone when they cried for bread. The Universities could supply instead the right kind of teaching and the right kind of teachers. Their high position would cause "the scheme to be favourably viewed, and enable it successfully to overcome those crotchets and oppositions which every new scheme has to encounter."

There were three kinds of objectors. There were those who said the Universities could not afford the money; those who argued that, if they established Extension teaching, the number of undergraduates would decline; and those who maintained that the University ought not to court rebuff by making over-sanguine proposals.

Professor Stuart answered them all. To the first he replied that he knew that University funds were not inexhaustible, but he did not fear on that point, because the nation had always shown itself ready to give and to transfer money into those hands which, it believed, would use it well and for truly national work. To the second he replied that, so far from diminishing the existing numbers of the University, Extension teaching would act as a feeder to it. To the third he replied that "in any scheme we must be prepared to meet with disappointments and in some quarters with want of response. . . . I believe," he continued, "that it is not only our duty to foster and encourage a demand for education wherever it exists, but, by the attitude we assume, to endeavour to call it up where it does not exist or has not the energy to express itself."

He was right in saying that University Extension would not be without its disappointments. He was also right in his prophecy that it would in no way lessen, but would rather tend to increase, the number of resident students. But his anticipation of national aid for the educational work of University Extension has not yet been fulfilled. The State has wisely helped the local colleges; it has not yet helped the local committees which are trying to secure as many as possible of the advantages of a local college for small towns.

Professor Stuart's letter led to a shower of memorials. To consider them, the University appointed a Syndicate in 1872.[1] The Syndicate at once undertook a systematic enquiry into the alleged demand for courses of University lectures. In the following year they reported in favour of adopting, for an experimental period, the new scheme. They made it, however, a condition that the requisite funds should be provided by the local authorities. Thus University Extension became an official fact.

<small>The First Programme of University Extension.</small>

Its promoters were, of course, to a certain extent in the dark. They could do no more than guess the real extent of the demand for lectures. While the scheme was only talked about, a great many people no doubt took a sanguine view of the desire of their neighbourhood for University teaching. Face to face with a formal offer, the acceptance of which involved a money payment, a certain proportion of the memorialists decided to content themselves with a less comprehensive programme than they had originally contemplated. As Professor Stuart has said,[2] "we started on too ambitious a scale and we had to suffer for it." The promoters had in their mind three different classes of persons: women, young men in the

---

[1] "The Calendar of Cambridge Local Lectures for 1880-81. Historical Sketch of the Progress of Local Lectures," p. 5.

[2] "Inaugural Address to the Second Summer Meeting of University Extension Students in Oxford, 1889," p. 33.

position of clerks or shop-assistants, and working-people. The first idea was to have in each town a course specially adapted for each of these classes, and delivered on different days. But this proved, in almost every case, too costly. The larger towns were naturally the first to avail themselves of the new proposals. They contained a greater number of leisured or educationally-minded people; they furnished a larger area from which to draw subscriptions. For some of these larger towns the full programme was not too ambitious, but for the smaller and poorer towns, after the first burst of enthusiasm had flagged, it was practically out of the question.

The fact was that in most places no really general demand for higher education existed. It had to be created almost everywhere, and in many towns the work has still to be done. In every place a few of the leading inhabitants, the majority, perhaps, of the professional classes, a fair number of tradesmen, and not a few working-men, were keenly alive to the value of the lectures which the University of Cambridge had decided to offer. There was abundant reason that their desire for higher education should be met; but the difficulty was that there were so few people who really felt the desire. Without the assistance of others, they could hardly be expected to support the considerable expense of the full programme of lectures. However, the establishment of University Extension teaching stimulated such people everywhere. It made them eager to secure its advantages for their own town. Perhaps, in some cases, they overestimated the public interest in the work; but it was even a gain that they should realise the facts. Many *The Difficulties which it encountered.*

persons, when they discovered how languid an interest was taken by their fellow-citizens in higher education, set to work to put things right. And thus in a sense University Extension was instrumental in forming in many towns a kind of educational garrison.

But in a few of the larger towns a more complete programme could be at once adopted. The Durham College of Natural Science had been founded at Newcastle-on-Tyne in 1871. Three years later the Yorkshire College at Leeds was established under the title of the "Yorkshire College of Science," and in 1877, on the discontinuance of the Cambridge University Extension lectures, which had been given in Leeds since 1871, the College undertook the preparation of students for degrees in Arts. Mason College, Birmingham, was founded in 1875, University College, Bristol, was established in 1876, and University College, Liverpool, in 1878. Finally, as a direct outcome of the Cambridge University Extension lectures, Firth College, Sheffield, was founded, by the generosity of Mr. Mark Firth, in 1879, and University College, Nottingham, in 1881.

It is, of course, far from being the case that the establishment of all these colleges was due only to University Extension. They were the outcome of the same general movement of which University Extension is only one of the expressions. But, at the same time, there can be no doubt that the local supporters of these great institutions found in the new efforts of the Universities, if not direct assistance, at all events stimulus and encouragement.

In the foundation of one of these local colleges,

Oxford took a prominent part. This was in the case of University College, Bristol. The movement for the establishment of that college began among the inhabitants of Bristol themselves; and to aid this movement, two Oxford Colleges (New College and Balliol) offered to give £300 a year for five years.[1]

In the meantime something had been done in London. In 1876 a society was formed there, under the presidency of Mr. Goschen, for the Extension of University teaching, the three Universities, Oxford, Cambridge, and London, consenting to send representatives to a joint board, the functions of which were to advise the council of the society on educational matters. This society, through the efforts of its successive secretaries, Mr. Myers, Mr. E. T. Cook, and Dr. R. D. Roberts, has had an important and prosperous history, and is now one of the three great branches of the University Extension movement in England. *The Foundation of the London University Extension Society.*

The question of University Extension teaching was brought before the Oxford Commission of 1877 by Mr. Jowett (now Master of Balliol). He pointed out "the considerable movement for secondary adult education then going on in the large towns," and urged that the Universities should "take a little pains" about it. In conclusion he made two practical proposals to the Commissioners: "one that there should be an office for University Extension and a secretary paid by the University; and the other that the tenure of non-resident fellowships should be capable of *Commencement of the work by the University of Oxford.*

[1] University of Oxford Commission, Oct., 1877. Minutes of Evidence of Rev. B. Jowett, p. 155.

extension in the case of persons lecturing or holding professorships in the large towns."[1]

The year after Mr. Jowett gave his evidence, the University of Oxford offered for the first time to make arrangements for University Extension lectures on its own account. As had been the case five years before in Cambridge, the University supplemented its machinery for Local Examinations by a system of Local Lectures, while, by a happy coincidence, the Delegates appointed as their secretary for this new purpose Mr. Arthur Acland, whose father had been chiefly instrumental in framing the parent-system of Local Examinations.

The new scheme was now fairly launched. There followed a period of somewhat slow growth. In some places the new ground was ready for the new work. Here there was small difficulty. But in most towns it was an up-hill fight to keep the courses going. In many the work flickered, and then for a time went out. For the great majority of towns in England, University Extension was before its time. And this was especially true of the less populous manufacturing centres and the smaller country towns. It became clear that all towns were not ready for the same dose of University Extension teaching, and that some could only take it in homœopathic quantities.

There was need, therefore, for two things: for patience to wait until the public mind had caught the desire for University Extension courses, and for some readjustment of the system, in order to make it more available for the smaller towns and the poorer districts of large ones. The experience,

[1] University of Oxford Commission, Oct., 1877. Minutes of Evidence of Rev. B. Jowett, p. 155.

however, gained in the first ten years of University Extension threw light on the best ways of overcoming the difficulties which thus impeded its further development.

It was obvious that University Extension must be made cheaper. Many towns, which would gladly have tried the scheme, shrank from the pecuniary liability which its adoption would involve. Some few places looked back ruefully on a previous deficit, and, generally speaking, such of the working-men's societies as possessed funds available for educational purposes, thought the lectures too dear. But the smaller towns and the poor districts of the larger cities were exactly the quarters in which many of the promoters of University Extension were most anxious that the movement should spread. In other words, financial difficulties hampered its growth on the two sides where growth was most needed. How could these difficulties be overcome? The fees paid to the lecturers could not be reduced, if the services of the right kind of men were to be retained: local expenses had already been brought down to the lowest level. The one possible remedy was to offer shorter courses; to give localities, as it were, a sample of University Extension teaching. Such an arrangement would go far towards halving the cost, and would enable the poorer centres to make a beginning. It would also make it easier for a small group of earnest students, themselves unable to meet the expense of a longer course, to raise in their locality subscriptions to the necessary amount. A few poor students, who would despair of begging guarantees for an outlay of £60, would attack in good heart the smaller task of raising £30. And it was felt that the local committees might be safely trusted to work their way up to the longer course, with its proportionately heavier expenses, when they had once contrived to make both ends meet in the smaller venture. For, if University Extension teaching was a good thing and suited to local needs, it seemed obvious that the local committees would soon desire a larger measure of it.

<small>The New Departure in 1885.</small>

This system of shorter courses had been, it is true, occasionally employed before, but its bold adoption practically dates from the autumn of 1885. In that year the whole movement started forward. Oxford began work on a larger scale, its new vigour being largely owing to the initiative of the present Headmaster of Rugby, then President of Trinity College. A conspicuous feature of the Oxford work was its employment of the short course system. There were naturally serious objections to the policy. Half a loaf may be better than no bread, but towns which can afford a complete system of teaching need not be encouraged to content themselves with one that is incomplete. The offer of a shorter course might relax energies which were really capable of securing a full one. It is undeniable that there was great weight in this view of the question. However, the policy of offering short courses has been amply justified by its results. It has practically brought University Extension within the reach of every town in England.

<small>The Oxford "Travelling Libraries" and Summer Meeting.</small>

Oxford has added two other leading features to the work. It began the system of Travelling Libraries in 1885, and it started the Summer Meeting in 1888. A great difficulty with many University Extension students is that books of reference bearing on the subjects of the courses of lectures are not accessible to them. They are not all within reach of good public or private libraries. It was a good thing to send down to each lecture-centre a fair selection of the books recommended by the lecturer for study during his course.[1] The idea of a general Summer Meeting of University Extension students was derived from the assembly held at Chautauqua in the United States. The application of the idea to English conditions was due to a suggestion made by Mr. Charles Rowley of Manchester to a small committee which, at the instance of Dr. Paton of Nottingham, had met to consider the possibility of introducing into England a system of Reading Circles, similar in point of arrangement to those which centre in the assembly at Chautauqua.

It was at once felt that, by means of a Summer Meeting in one of the University towns, the Extension movement would be able to avail itself of the services of those resident teachers who, though friendly to the work, are prevented by their University duties from taking any active part in it as lecturers. The plan would furnish an opportunity for an excellent use of the scholarships previously offered by Mr. J. G. Talbot, M.P., and others to enable deserving University Extension students to reside in Oxford for a short period of vacation study. The students would enjoy the great advantage offered by the University museums, collections, and libraries, and would gain stimulus

[1] The form of the boxes in which the books are packed was taken from those used for a similar purpose by the Yorkshire Union of Mechanics' Institutes.

from their intercourse with one another. In short, the Meeting would introduce into University Extension the one element in which, from the University point of view, it had been chiefly lacking—the element of "residence."

The idea of the Summer Meeting was at once taken up in Oxford, where already, on a small scale, arrangements had been made during the Long Vacations of some previous years for the accommodation, within College walls, of elementary schoolmasters and others. The details of the programme for a large meeting of students were worked out in the Oxford Extension Office, and finally, under the joint supervision of the Delegates and a special committee of residents, the first University Extension Summer Meeting was held in August, 1888. Another and still more successful meeting followed in 1889, and in 1890 Oxford held its third Summer Meeting—Cambridge also venturing on a similar experiment, though on a smaller scale. Both Universities have held Meetings in August of the present year (1891), the Cambridge Meeting being still limited in numbers to about sixty students, while the attendance at the Oxford Meeting was much larger than on any previous occasion.

An Anticipation of the Idea of the Summer Meeting.

It is interesting to note that, just as Mr. Sewell in 1850 had virtually anticipated the idea of University Extension teaching, so another writer had made a happy forecast of the Summer Meeting. In a letter to the *Times* of October 15, 1874, the Rev. E. S. Ffoulkes, the Vicar of St. Mary's, Oxford, wrote as follows:—

"The practical account of the matter is that Oxford is wanted by the University for *six* months in the year, and no more. Why, then, should Oxford be debarred from accommodating another University for the remaining six? It would be a vast saving to the nation if the same buildings which serve for one University could serve for two. . . . Or ladies might be invited to form themselves into a University for six months. Or, again, to suggest the form which would involve least change, why should not candidates for the Local Examinations be given the option of a residence in College rooms, under proper surveillance, for the four summer months which constitute the Long Vacation, to prepare for their examinations? It is quite possible that numbers of middle-class men would only be too glad to avail themselves of a University curriculum, could it be achieved by four months' residence continuously during the summer. Oxford could easily be provided with a staff of Tutors and Professors from its existing University to officer a second. And how cheap and how productive of work would that term be, which lasted a period of four months without a break, and whose days were such as to need neither coal nor candle, nor other light than that of the sun, to give twelve hours of study. . . . Positively the only change which this would necessitate would be that colleges should let their rooms *furnished*, so as to have them at their disposal for the whole year."

It remains to add a short account of the developments which have taken place since the issue (in August, 1890) of the last edition of this book. Of the new departure in connection with the County Council grants—an advance which promises to have a deep influence on the future development of University Extension work—we shall give a full account in the next chapter. In the same place also it will be more appropriate to give a detailed description of the changes made in the arrangement of the studies undertaken at the Oxford Summer Meeting—changes which, by grouping the courses into sequences extending over four years, have given an almost

Developments during the past Year, 1890-91.

County Council Lectures.

Four Years' Sequence of Studies at the Oxford Summer Meeting.

entirely new character and value to that branch of the system. It remains for us to allude to the recent and successful attempts made by the Oxford, Cambridge, and London lecturers to organise themselves by means of a "Lecturers' Association." To this new Association everyone interested in the University Extension movement will heartily wish success. Much of the future efficiency of the system will depend on the continuance of the hearty co-operation between the lecturers and the central offices, and on the careful consideration by the lecturers of the varied and difficult problems which, especially in a period of rapid growth, come up with increasing frequency for discussion and settlement. The new Association will, no doubt, be able to furnish valuable suggestions to the central authorities, and in many ways to contribute to the general well-being of the system. It is also to be noted that an indirect effect of the work of the Association will be to make the lecturers who are attached to the several branches of the system personally acquainted with one another, and thus to promote the unity of the movement.

Lecturers' Association.

But by far the most striking advance of the year 1890-91 has been made in America. A year ago, in the first two editions of this book, the statement that "in the last five years University Extension has been started in Scotland, in Ireland, in America, and in Australia" seemed an adequate reference to the transatlantic movement. With characteristic enthusiasm and energy—helped, no doubt, by the easier conditions offered by the new country, and by the experience gathered in the old—Pennsylvania and New York have, in a single session, done such

University Extension in America.

work as entitles them to rank with the Oxford, Cambridge, and London organisations. We, in England, owe the conception of our Summer Meetings to Chautauqua, and we note, therefore, with the greatest pleasure the generosity with which our American friends seize every opportunity of tracing the local lecture system to its first home in our island. The idea of taking the University to the people is English, that of bringing the people together into a Vacation University is American. These are the two central features of University Extension as it now exists. The great leap forward in the English movement during the last three or four years is undoubtedly in large measure due to their combination. The local centres do the preparatory work, and furnish the constituency for our Summer Meetings; the Summer Meetings in turn have drawn the isolated centres together, have imparted *esprit de corps* to the students, and have demonstrated the national character of the movement. A very large proportion of the newer centres owe their origin to the missionary spirit caught at the Summer Meetings. Everyone must hope that, with so satisfactory a growth resulting from the cross-fertilisation of English and American ideas, the movement, international in its origin, may remain international in its history.

The rapidity of the development in the United States and the distance which separates us from them make it difficult, as yet, to give an adequate account of what has taken place. In the near future the writers hope to have an opportunity of making enquiries on the spot. The following, however, seem to be the salient dates and the names which most merit record.

In America, as in England, other movements had done much to ripen the demand for the general diffusion of higher education. The Lyceums of New England, the counterparts of our Mechanics' Institutes and Literary and Philosophical Societies, were at work half a century ago. More recently the Chautauqua University was started, and it was apparently in the State of New York, which contains Chautauqua, that lectures avowedly on the University Extension plan were first organised.[1] In the winter of 1887-88, a course on economics was delivered at Buffalo, under the auspices of the Buffalo Public Library, to audiences averaging from 200 to 250, and composed of "working-men, business men, professional men, ladies, and school-pupils." A class of an hour's duration was held after each lecture. In the winter of 1888-89 the experiment was repeated, the subject chosen being American history. At the same time Chautauqua set about organising a system of local lectures,[2] and, what is very striking, adopted at once the two ideas which Oxford had already contributed to the movement: the special training of young lecturers, and the system of travelling libraries for use in connection with the local lectures. The Chautauquans were fortunate in securing as one of their leaders Prof. H. B. Adams, of Johns Hopkins University, who

[1] For an account of the various American movements which show the spirit of University Extension, but which preceded the conscious adoption of the English idea, see Prof. H. B. Adams's excellent article on "University Extension" in the American edition of the *Review of Reviews* for July, 1891.

[2] Having in the previous autumn issued a circular, which did much to spread a knowledge of the aims and methods of the movement.

apparently, by the common consent of all Americans engaged in the work, has been the foremost pioneer "in helping the Cambridge and Oxford idea to take root in our soil." At about the same time Mr. Seth T. Stewart, supported by prominent professors of Harvard, Yale, Princeton, and Columbia Colleges, established the "University and School Extension," with its headquarters at Brooklyn. On July 9, 1889, Mr. Melvil Dewey read a paper before the Convocation of the University of the State of New York, which may truly be described as epoch-making. He pictured University Extension in the largest sense of the words, told the history and methods of the English movement, recounted the attempts already made in America, and asked that the University should embark on the task of extending itself. Next day the Regents of the University met, and passed a series of resolutions, adopting some of his suggestions at once, and assigning others to committees for enquiry.

So far we have had to chronicle chiefly preparation and experiments, and these in the main concentrated in the State of New York. The idea was, however, spreading into other regions, and in February, 1890, took root at Philadelphia, now the seat of the American Society for the Extension of University Teaching. A meeting of the leading educational authorities of the city was summoned by Provost Pepper of the University of Pennsylvania, and the result of the discussion which took place in his house, and of subsequent agitation, was the foundation in June, 1890, of the Philadelphia Society for the Extension of University Teaching. Mr. Henderson was appointed its secretary, and was at once "sent to study the system as organised in Oxford, Cambridge, and London." In the following month many of the leaders of the English movement had the pleasure of receiving visits from Mr. Melvil Dewey and Mr. Henderson. The first local centre at Philadelphia was opened on November 3, with a course on chemistry, and so energetically was the work of organisation carried forward that the Society have been able to announce recently that "during the first season (from November 1, 1890, to May 1, 1891) there were established twenty-three centres, where over forty courses of lectures were delivered to a total audience of nearly 60,000."[1] It happened that last winter the well-known Cambridge Extension lecturer, Mr. R. G. Moulton, was in America on a lecturing tour. Having observed the excellent spirit of the work commenced at Philadelphia, Mr. Moulton returned there after Christmas, when his other engagements were completed, and, placing himself at the disposal of the society, contributed powerfully to the initial success which has been achieved.

In December, 1890, the Philadelphian organisers established the American Society for the Extension of University Teaching, and the Philadelphian Society became its first branch. The object of the national society is to disseminate throughout the land the information which the Philadelphians have had to obtain direct from England, and to afford means for the interchange of experience

[1] A number apparently arrived at by adding together the numbers attending *each lecture*.' If so, it is not comparable with the English statistics, which give the *average* attendance at *each course* of lectures.

obtained in different localities. The first number of its new monthly journal, *University Extension*, was published on July 1 of the present year.

New York, which has thus allowed itself to be temporarily outstripped by its neighbour, has made preparations for a campaign during the coming winter which bids fair to produce some remarkable results. It has taken a step in advance of the mother movement on this side of the ocean by obtaining from the State Legislature a grant of $10,000, which is not confined to technical education. This action has been largely due to the persistent and enthusiastic efforts of Mr. Dewey and to the supply of pamphlets maintained by the American Society. The history of the passing of the Bill will amuse those accustomed to English Parliamentary methods. To staid Europeans it reads almost as though the nation were in the throes of some great crisis requiring immediate remedies. On April 14, 1891, the Senate unanimously passed the "University Extension Bill." On the 15th the Ways and Means Committee of the Assembly unanimously agreed to report it favourably. On the 16th it was passed unanimously by the Assembly. We here reproduce this first University Extension Law, which, it should be remarked, is no parochial bye-law, but the enactment of a State almost as large as England without Wales and as populous as Belgium.

THE UNIVERSITY EXTENSION LAW.
AN ACT TO PROMOTE WIDER EXTENSION TO THE PEOPLE OF OPPORTUNITIES FOR EDUCATION.

The People of the State of New York, represented in Senate and Assembly, do enact as follows:—

§ 1. To provide for, promote, more widely extend to, and

bring within the reach of the people at large, adults as well as youth, opportunities and facilities for education, the regents of the University of the State of New York are hereby authorised to co-operate with localities, organisations and associations in this State, where such education shall be desired, and to aid therein by recommending methods therefor, designating suitable persons as instructors, conducting examinations, granting certificates thereupon, and otherwise rendering assistance in such educational work.

§ 2. The sum of $10,000, or so much thereof as may be necessary, is hereby appropriated from any money in the treasury not otherwise appropriated, for the necessary expenses of carrying into effect the provisions of this Act, said expenses to be paid by the treasurer on the warrant of the comptroller, on vouchers duly authenticated by the regents of the University; but no part of the sum herein appropriated shall be expended in paying for the services or expenses of persons designated or appointed as lecturers or instructors to carry out the provisions of this Act; it being the intent of this Act that such expenses shall be borne by the localities benefited.

§ 3. This Act shall take effect immediately.

It will be noted that the law authorises a grant to the central body, the University of the State, apparently for the purposes chiefly of organisation. In England the costs of the central offices are already largely borne by Universities, which are not dependent on the State, and many other circumstances make it desirable that the State's aid should be assigned to other portions of the work. While the general aim and methods of the two movements are identical, it is clear that their advance must often follow different roads, owing to the difference of the national institutions. It is for these reasons that in the chapters on the present and the future we confine our attention to the English schemes, with whose conditions and working alone we are personally familiar.

In the last two or three months University Extension Societies have been inaugurated in many of the large towns of America, and Extension departments organised in connection with many Universities. Within one week, says *University Extension*, the movement was a leading subject of discussion at five great gatherings, at Bedford (Pa.), at Ocean City (Md.), at Chautauqua, at Albany, and at Toronto. An elaborate system of University Extension is one of the constituent parts of the new University of Chicago.[1]

We have now traced the history of University Extension from its first beginnings to its present form. So short a sketch of so varied a movement must necessarily be incomplete. A great debt is owing to many workers whose labours and whose names cannot even be mentioned here; but enough has been said to show how naturally the whole system has grown up in our midst. One change has led to another; each development seems to have suggested a further one. The extension of the advantages of University teaching to one class brought about its further extension to a second; the machinery of local examinations seemed naturally to lend itself to the purposes of local lectures.

Conclusion: The natural Character of the Developments of University Extension.

It could hardly have been otherwise; for it was inevitable that, the more the country came to care for education, the heavier would be the claims made on the activity and the resources of the Uni-

[1] This account of University Extension in America is based on Prof. H. B. Adams's paper in the *Review of Reviews*, on Mr. Melvil Dewey's paper before the Convocation of the University of the State of New York; on the first number of the journal *University Extension* and on various pamphlets and circulars issued chiefly from New York and Philadelphia.

versities as representative of the highest education in the land. The movement has gone forward without serious check. The area of its operations has been very greatly extended, and the methods of its organisation have been in all departments improved.

TABLE SHOWING THE ADVANCE MADE IN THE WORK OF UNIVERSITY EXTENSION DURING THE LAST SIX YEARS.

	OXFORD.	CAMBRIDGE.	LONDON.	TOTAL.
Courses delivered [1] :—				
1885–1886	27	82	63	172
1890–1891	192	135	130	457
Average attendances :—				
1885–1886	3,000	8,557	5,195	16,752
1890–1891	20,248	10,947	12,923	44,118

The two maps which follow show the local distribution of the advance during the same period of six years.

The two diagrams which are placed after the maps summarise two aspects of the entire history of the English movement. The curves show the first rapid rise of the Cambridge system, the subsequent sudden fall in numbers, perhaps partly due to the absorption of some of the best centres into new local colleges, and then a gradual rise to about the same position as that gained in 1875. The

[1] In the case of London the numbers are for 1885 and 1890.

UNIVERSITY EXTENSION CENTRES, 1885-86.

■ Oxford Centres.   ○ Cambridge Centres.
  + Outlying London Centres.
The remaining London Centres were 29 in number.

UNIVERSITY EXTENSION CENTRES, 1890-91.

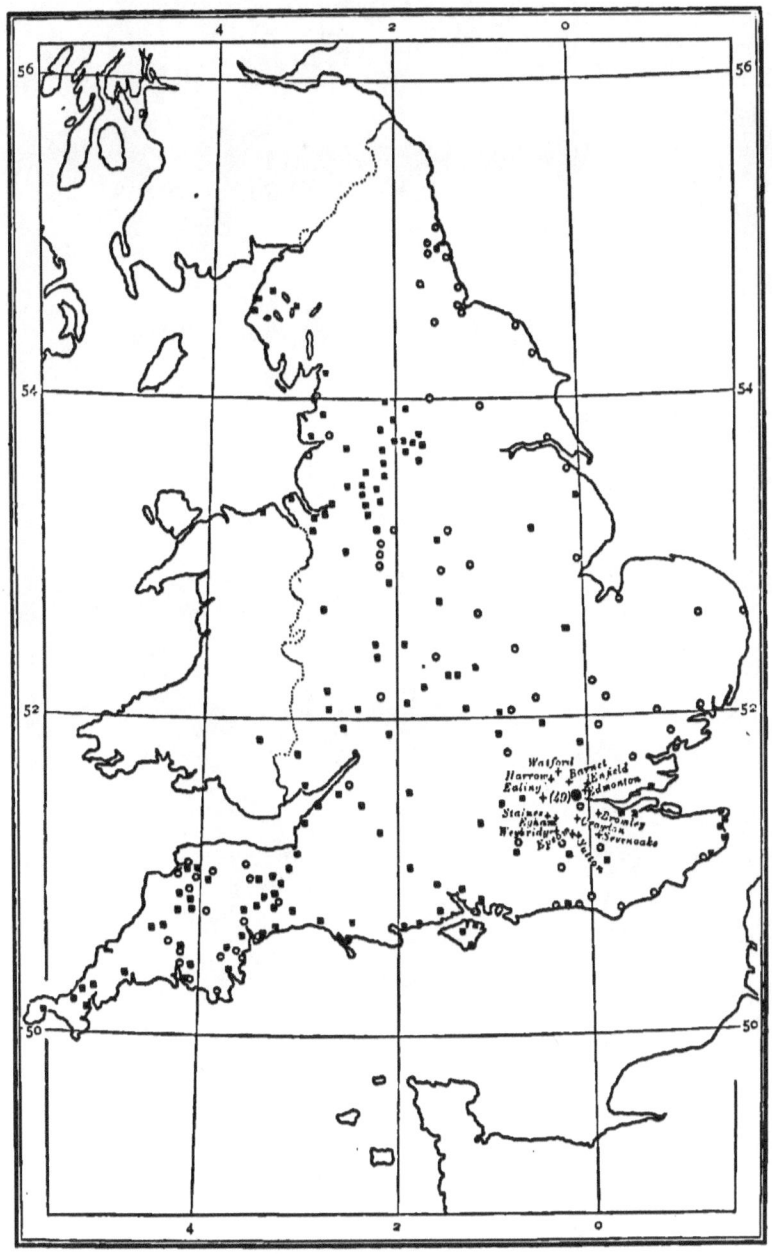

■ Oxford Centres.   ○ Cambridge Centres.
  + Outlying London Centres.
The remaining London Centres were 49 in number.

DIAGRAM SHOWING AVERAGE ATTENDANCE AT COURSES OF LECTURES.

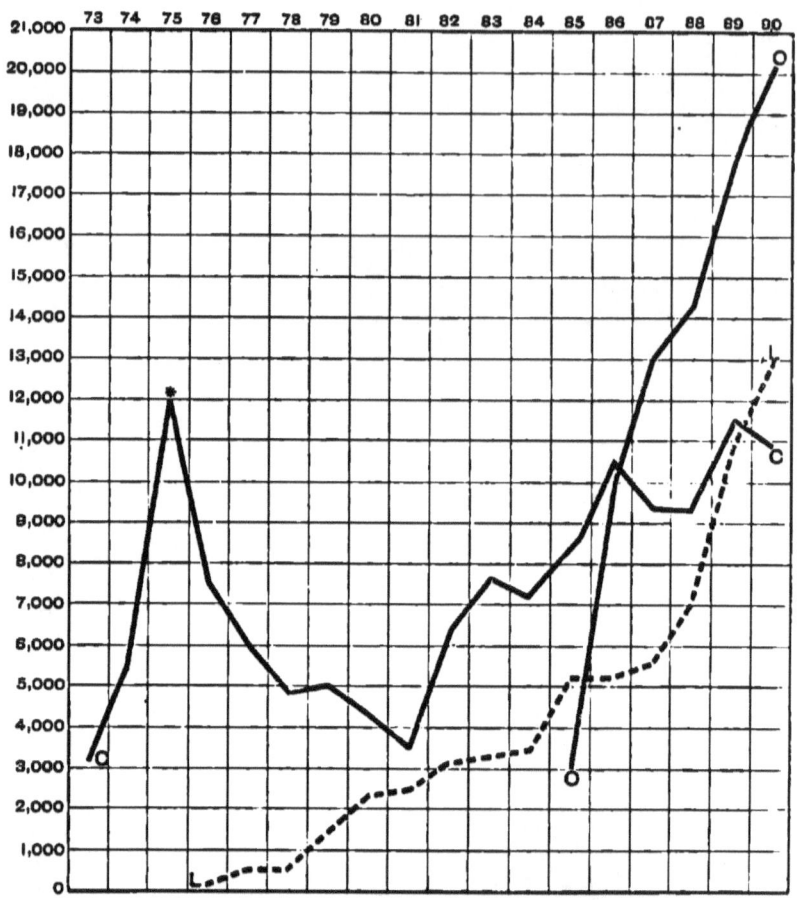

———— Oxford (o) and Cambridge (c).—Average Attendance at Courses.
- - - - - London (L).—Entries for Courses.
* The number for this year is estimated, the records being incomplete.

DIAGRAM SHOWING RESULTS OF EXAMINATIONS.

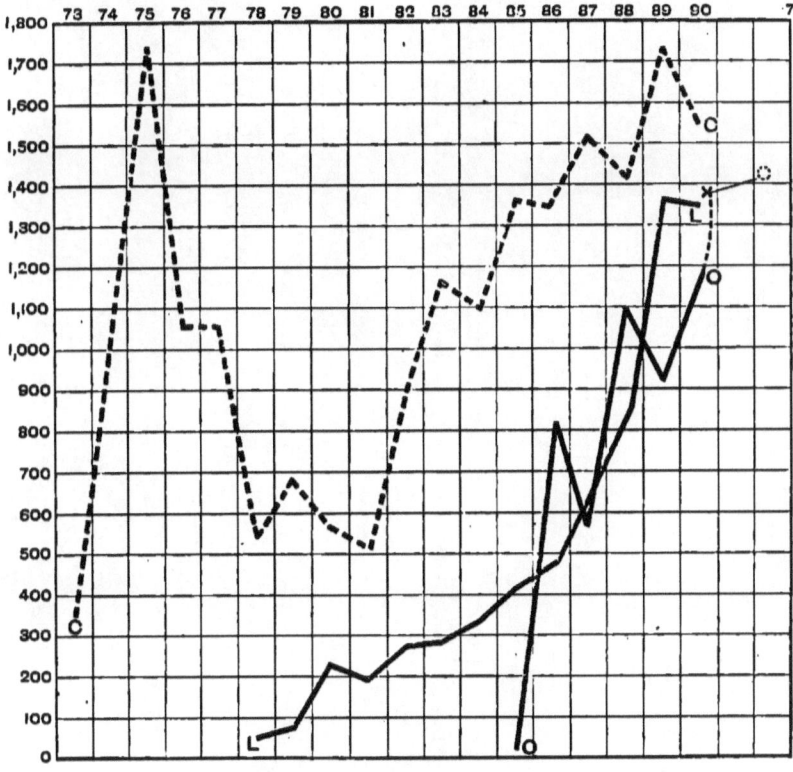

- - - - Number Examined.
———— Number of Certificates awarded.
×   Number Examined by Oxford in 1890-91.
O Oxford.   C Cambridge.   L London.

London curves indicate a steady progress, slow at first, more rapid afterwards, when the People's Lectures began to feed the regular courses with students. The Oxford curves show that branch of the work to have quickly surpassed the Cambridge and London branches in the matter of attendance; but, as regards examinations, to be only now beginning to rival them. Of the two striking drops (in 1887 and 1889) in the number of certificates awarded by Oxford, one at least was due to the raising of the standard of examination, so that it might be comparable with that of well-known University examinations. According to the instructions now issued to the examiners, a pass certificate is to be awarded where the candidate's work is *pro tanto* up to the standard of a " pass school " at Oxford; a certificate of distinction, where the pupil's work shows knowledge and ability such as, if exhibited in a necessary proportion of papers, would earn a class in an " honour school." On a later page we quote on this point from the reports of the examiners.

Owing to differences in the methods of compilation, the statistics available for Oxford, Cambridge, and London are not quite comparable. This fact is indicated by differences in the character of the curves which mark the progress of the numbers.

CHAPTER II.

UNIVERSITY EXTENSION—THE PRESENT.

DURING the eighteen years which have elapsed since local lectures were first undertaken by the University of Cambridge, the words "University Extension" have obtained a narrower and more definite meaning than they originally possessed. They now denote a particular method of instruction and a particular system of organisation: both of them evolved to meet the special wants of a democratic age, and both of them, at any rate in their present form, fresh contributions to the art of education. Courses of instruction given by University graduates form the backbone of most systems of higher education; but University Extension lectures have several adjuncts intended to adapt them to non-academical conditions, and to correct the defects involved in all teaching by lecture. The syllabus, the class, the guided reading, the weekly exercise, the students' association and the final examination are almost as important elements in this system of instruction as the lecture itself. From the point of view of organisation, University Extension is designed to meet the requirements of elasticity, cheapness, and thoroughness—elasticity, by its "centres" managed by independent local committees, who gauge the varying wants and possibilities of different neighbourhoods; cheapness, by the system of peripatetic lecturers, each of whom divides his time among several "centres"; thoroughness, by the University control over the appointment both of lecturers and examiners.

A Typical Centre. We will commence our survey of University Extension as it exists to-day with the description of the foundation and working of a typical "centre." It usually owes its origin to one person of energy, very often to a lady, who, having seen the system at work elsewhere, determines to establish it in her own town. She interests her friends in the scheme, and most likely undertakes the burden of secretaryship herself. The mayor is then visited, and a public meeting called, which, it is announced, will be attended by a representative of one of the Universities. Resolutions are passed, a committee is elected, and the appointment of the secretary is ratified. A house-to-house journey or an "at home" raises the list of guarantors. The committee meet to choose a lecturer and a subject. The secretary makes a formal application to one of the Central Offices, and if the lecturer applied for is free, dates are fixed and advertisement is commenced. The editors of the local newspapers are interested, and various members of the committee undertake to dispose of a certain number of tickets.

When the lecturer arrives for the first time he is taken to the house of one of the committee. He learns from his host the nature of the audience, and hears of many local difficulties and peculiarities. He delivers his inaugural lecture, organises his class, and explains the method and opportunities of the scheme. If he is successful, the doubtful are convinced, and the "course" is satisfactorily floated. The lectures are delivered at weekly or fortnightly intervals, and there are from six to twelve lectures in the course. A universal characteristic of Extension lectures is the syllabus—a pamphlet containing an analysis of each lecture, a list of text-books and other authorities on the subject, and such quotations and statistics as the lecturer finds it expedient to put into print. Wherever possible, the lectures are illustrated by specimens and diagrams. Owing to its intrinsic merits, and to the difficulty of carrying cumbersome diagrams and specimens about by train, the lantern is in growing favour as a means of illustration. In some cases the lecturer is able to make use of the local museum, and in the case of one or two courses on musical subjects, a local chorus has been trained for purposes of illustration. After each lecture there is an interval, during which some of the audience withdraw, leaving only the "students." A "class" is then held, during which the lecturer goes into further details and explains difficulties. The lecturer gets to know personally at least the more active and promising of his students. At each class questions are given out, on which the students write short essays. These "weekly (or fortnightly) papers" are regarded as one of the essential features of the system. They are usually sent to the lecturer by post, and he returns them at the following class bearing his corrections and comments. In the case of the Oxford lectures, a "travelling library" accompanies every course. It consists of a strong box containing about twenty or thirty of the books recommended by the lecturer, which are either lent in rotation to the students or deposited in some accessible room for reference.

At the close of the course, the lecturer prepares a list of those students who have attended at least a certain proportion—usually two-thirds or three-quarters—of the lectures and classes, and have written the same proportion of the "weekly papers." These students are qualified to sit for the examination which is held at the centre by the University authorities. Three weeks or a month after the last lecture, the examiner, who is appointed by the University and is other than the lecturer, issues a list of successful candidates, arranged in two classes, those who have gained "distinction," and those who have "satisfied the examiner." A prize is awarded to the student at the head of the list. At a later meeting, not unfrequently the first lecture of a subsequent course, the member of Parliament or some other local magnate distributes the certificates and gives away the prizes.

Of course there are many variations from the typical centre. In some cases the course is arranged and the payment of the University account is guaranteed by some already existing society, a Mechanics' Institute, a Local College, or a Public Library; occasionally even by a wealthy individual. The working-men's centres in the north of England are, in several instances, organised by co-operative societies. In all cases, however, the essential parts of the local organisation are the Local Secretary, who maintains touch with the Central University Office, and the person or persons who guarantee the payment of the University bill. *Variations from the Typical Centre.*

Such is, at present, the normal character of the local institutions of the University Extension system. There are, however, abundant signs of *Approaching changes in Local Organisation.*

approaching changes in their constitution, which will have the effect of wholly altering the status of the movement. From a loose federation of private societies, University Extension is rising to the position of a national organisation, led indeed by the old Universities, but recognised and aided by the State. So rapid a growth cannot take place without calling for great efforts on the part of the local organisers, and one of the best results of the past years of struggle, and of the many conferences held recently at Oxford, at Cambridge, and in London, has been the training of a body of local secretaries, who in many instances have won the confidence of the University Authorities, and are gaining marked authority in their own neighbourhoods. As the system increases in complexity, and as its aims become of necessity less simple than they have been, it will more and more depend on these secretaries, and on others locally associated with them, to originate the institutions best suited to the local conditions. The changes which have already commenced, and in which local organisers have taken a considerable part, are chiefly the federation of the centres in different districts, the "municipalisation" of certain centres, and the formation of groups of country centres for the teaching of technical science in connection with several of the County Councils.

The District Federations. The greatest advantage which has as yet come from the formation of the District Federations or Associations has been of a social nature. The personal acquaintance of neighbouring local secretaries materially smoothes the difficulties of organisation, as, for instance, by breaking down the barrier which has too often separated the

Oxford and the Cambridge centres. Both Universities have offered reduced terms to federations which can form convenient circuits for the lecturers, but as yet it cannot be said that up to the present year the direct action of these bodies had done much in the way of easing the burden of the central offices. By electing officers, however, who are entitled to speak as the District or County leaders of the movement, the Associations have fully vindicated their existence, and have greatly facilitated the recent negotiations with the County Councils of Devon, Kent, Yorkshire, and Lancashire. There can be no question that their duties and powers will accumulate in the future, and that the centres of the Midlands and the Eastern Counties would do well to follow the example of the North and the South, by forming similar leagues. The following is a list of the Associations already formed arranged in the order in which they arose, and the names and addresses of their secretaries :—

South-Eastern Counties Association (Kent, Surrey, Sussex, and Hampshire)	Hon. Sec.	Rev. H. E. B. Arnold, St. Matthew's Vicarage, Oakley Square, London, N.W.
	Hon. Assist. Sec.	A. Rawlings, Esq., High Street, Guildford.
South-Western Counties Association (Cornwall, Devon, and Somerset)	Hon. Secs.	Miss B. Vivian, Reskadinnick, Camborne.
Yorkshire Association	Gen. Hon. Sec.	Edward J. Wilson, Esq., 6, Whitefriar Gate, Hull.
	Hon. Sec. for Oxford Centres.	Miss Snowdon, Riddings Road, Ilkley.
Lancashire and Cheshire Association	Hon. Secs.	J. H. Fowler, Esq., Holyrood, Prestwich, Manchester. J. C. Gray, Esq, Co-operative Union, Corporation Street, Manchester.

The most striking effort yet made to "municipalise" a centre is that now in progress at Exeter. It is due, in the first instance, to a suggestion made by the writers, but if it succeeds,

"Municipalisation" of Local Centres.

the chief credit will belong to Miss Montgomery, the able and energetic local secretary at Exeter, one of the finest centres in the country. The following resolutions, passed by the local committee, speak for themselves; but we direct especial attention to the fifth, which, containing as it does the old constitutional principle of representation accompanying taxation, is worthy of serious consideration on the part of all local organisers :—

Resolutions passed by the Exeter Executive Committee (being themselves all Subscribers).

1. That the Mayor be *ex-officio* President.

2. That the following be appointed Vice-Presidents: The Bishop, Sir Stafford Northcote, M.P., Sir Thomas Acland (and five other gentlemen well known in the city).

3. That the following public bodies be asked to directly appoint representatives on the Committee :—
   The City Council—nine members.[1]
   The Subscribers—nine.
   The School Board—one.
   The Cathedral Body—one.
   The Museum Committee—two.
   The Literary Society—two.
   The Devon and Exeter Institution—two.
   The Chamber of Commerce—one.
   The Working Men's Society—one.
   The Co-operative Society—one.

4. That the following be *ex-officio* members of the Committee :—
   The Chairman of the Technical Education Committee of the County Council; the Principal of the Training College; the Head-Master and Head-Mistresses of the four chief Schools; the Hon. Secretaries for Oxford and Cambridge Local Examinations; and the Hon. Treasurer and Secretary of the University Extension Committee.

5. That it be distinctly understood that all members of

[1] The City Council has recently appointed its representatives and voted a proportionate contribution.

the Committee must be subscribers; or that the body they represent must subscribe out of its funds in proportion to the number of representatives.

6. That the present Committee be empowered to act until the new one be appointed.

In a communication to the *Oxford University Extension Gazette*, Miss Montgomery, after recording the above resolutions, goes on to say :—

"We hope that by these changes we may reach large bodies of people, and give them a direct share and interest in our work. They will certainly make our Committee the most widely representative body in the city, so that if we are entrusted with money either from the funds at the disposal of the Town Council for Technical Instruction, or from the Treasury, we shall be in all respects a body fit to deal with public money, since we shall represent not any particular section of the inhabitants, but *all* classes and *all* occupations."

More important, however, either than the District Associations or the municipalisation of the centres has been the influence of the "spirit money," "ear-marked" for technical education, which unexpectedly fell into the hands of County Councils about a year ago. The first edition of this little book was written immediately after Mr. Goschen, as Chancellor of the Exchequer, had, on July 21, 1890, proposed to the House of Commons "to add the amount set free by the abandonment of the licensing clauses to the residue which under the Bill as it stands goes to the County Councils, accompanying this inclusion by an intimation that possibly new charges may by-and-by be put upon them in reference to intermediate, technical, and agricultural education. It seems desirable, if more is to be done in this respect, that the localities, especially County Councils, should be interested in the work."

Technical Education and the County Council.

E

The Local Taxation Act of 1890, which partially embodied these proposals, made no reference to general intermediate education for England, but allowed the County Councils to apply the money "for the purposes of technical instruction within the meaning of the Technical Instruction Act of 1889." The definition of Technical Instruction in the latter Act is peculiar :—

"Technical Instruction shall mean instruction in the principles of science and art applicable to industries, and in the application of special branches of science and art to specific industries and employments. It shall not include the teaching the practice of any trade, industry, or employment, but shall include instruction in the branches of *science and art*, with respect to which grants are, for the time being, made by the Department of Science and Art, and *any other form of instruction* (*including modern languages and commercial and agricultural subjects*) which may, for the time being, be sanctioned by the Department by a minute laid before Parliament, and made on the representation of a local authority that such a form of instruction is required by the circumstances of its district."

As the discretion here given to the Department of Science and Art has been liberally interpreted, it has gradually become clear that the County Councils may aid financially the teaching of any subjects except History and Literature. There are even those who would find in the last words of the clause justification under certain circumstances for the teaching of History and Literature, but the whole context seems to show clearly that this was not the intention of the Legislature.

During the past winter the great majority of the County Councils have been busily endeavouring to avail themselves of the powers given to them by Parliament, but, as was foreseen, have been somewhat bewildered by the prospect of having to create every detail of the necessary machinery. Under the circumstances several of them have turned to the Universities, and have sought to adapt University Extension organisation and methods to the new purposes of the so-called technical education.[1] Devon and Norfolk were the scenes of the chief experiments in this direction, which were undertaken in the early months of the present year. In Devonshire courses of instruction on elementary chemistry and mechanics, with especial reference to agriculture, were given by Oxford and Cambridge graduates in thirty-seven small towns and large villages. The following table gives the general results obtained by this hastily-organised effort:—

	Average Attendance.	Certificates Awarded.	
		Pass.	Distinction.
Oxford Courses	968	73	48
Cambridge Courses	483	30	14
	1,451	103	62

In the county of Norfolk another plan was tried, under the superintendence of the University of Cambridge. The instruction was in this case given to about 130 elementary school teachers. The county was divided into three districts, with Norwich, King's Lynn, and Elmham as centres.

[1] We are far from thinking that the University Extension system should seek to undertake more than its due share of the new work of Technical Education, which will tax the resources of all the Institutions able to supply teachers, experience or direction.

Here the teachers gathered every Saturday by train. Lectures were given on the elementary principles of Chemistry, with special reference to their application to Agriculture. Each lecture was followed by a course of practical work, when the teachers themselves performed the more important experiments. The report of the Cambridge Syndicate states that—"It is intended that such of the teachers as are considered qualified by knowledge and ability should be appointed in the autumn to give village lectures. These teachers will be supplied with sets of ordinary apparatus by the County Council, and the more costly apparatus will be kept at a central institution from which the teachers may borrow as occasion requires."

During the past summer the Oxfordshire County Council has arranged similar courses for elementary teachers at Oxford, though not in connection with the Extension office. The Devonshire plan, with more or less of variation in details, is to be followed during the coming winter by the County Councils of Devon, Surrey, and Kent in connection with Oxford and Cambridge, by the County Councils of Somerset, Shropshire, Notts, and Oxfordshire in connection with Oxford only, and by the County Council of Cambridgeshire in connection with Cambridge only. Other counties are making arrangements with various local colleges. All the central institutions intend following up the preliminary instruction in Chemistry and Mechanics by teaching on such subjects as Agricultural Geology, Mining, Botany, Injurious Insects, Physiology of Farm Animals, and Hygiene both in reference to man and to domestic animals.

When a year ago we concluded the first

edition of this book by asking "that, when the educational institutions to which the County Councils may vote grants in aid come to be enumerated in an Act of Parliament, a prominent place may be given to University Extension," we had no idea that the effect of the Bill which was actually to pass through Parliament would be to give a one-sided endowment to much University Extension teaching. From the expression originally used by the Chancellor of the Exchequer—"*intermediate*, technical and agricultural education"—we had hoped otherwise. The danger which now threatens the less "paying" subjects of History and Literature, so important to the training of good citizens, is obvious. The authorities in University Extension have, however, felt it their duty to take their share in supplying the wants of the County Councils, that they might help in averting the very serious danger which threatens the best interests of all education in the present crisis—the danger of a divorce between technical and general education. If general education is organised by one set of authorities, and technical education left completely to another, there will arise a competition between them, and ultimately a conflict of vested interests, which will be deeply injurious to both. Rigid technical education, apart from the general principles of science and art, is likely to do more harm than good, by stereotyping present methods instead of leaving the power of rapid and intelligent adaption to our ever changing conditions.[1] General

---

[1] The forces constantly working in favour of practical instruction not based on scientific principles have become apparent, even in the first experiments of the County Councils, as is indicated by the following sentence from the Report of the Cam-

education, in this country at any rate, has already suffered by its too academical character, by its want of touch with life. While, however, the Universities cannot undertake the teaching of handicraft—a very important branch of technical education, to which many of the County Councils are rightly devoting much of the funds at their disposal—we believe that no other bodies can give the training in the general principles of science and art with more advantage both to themselves and to the community. And we believe that the danger of the neglect of History and Literature has only to be impressed on the public to bring about the changes necessary to avert the development of a one-sided system of Education.[1]

The Four Central Authorities. Four different bodies carry on the central organisation of University Extension in England: the University of Oxford, the University of Cambridge, the London Society for the Extension of University Teaching, and the Victoria University. At Oxford, the managing authority is a Committee appointed for the purpose by the

bridge Syndicate on the working of the Devonshire scheme :—
"There was some natural, though not very reasonable, disappointment on the part of those who expected to be able at once to derive practical advantages from the Lecturer's instruction."

[1] In his recent pamphlet on "*County Councils and Technical Education,*" Mr. J. C. Buckmaster argues (p. 18) that "lectures by themselves are never to be highly valued as a means of education," and implies that he regards the use made of the University Extension system by the County Councils as a mistake. He overlooks the fact that the main characteristic of the University Extension method of teaching, as contrasted with that of the older institutions to which he refers, lies in its combination of the lecture with the class, the written exercise, the syllabus, and the final examination (*see* supra, p. 46). We also think that Mr. Buckmaster underrates the stimulative power of the lecture as one part of a system of popular education.

Delegacy of Local Examinations. At Cambridge, it is the Local Examinations and Lectures Syndicate. The Oxford Congregation elects the Delegacy,[1] the Cambridge Senate the Syndicate, so that both at Oxford and Cambridge University Extension is authorised by the general bodies of resident Masters of Arts. The London Society is governed by a Council, which, on educational matters, is assisted and advised by a Joint Board, consisting of three representatives of each of the Universities of Oxford, Cambridge, and London. The General Board of Studies of the Victoria University has a Committee for Local Lectures. Each of the four bodies entrusts the detailed management to a secretary, who, in the cases of Oxford, Cambridge, and London, has an office and clerks.

The chief function of each "Central Office" is to supply to the local centres competent lecturers and examiners.

Within the Metropolitan Postal District. the London Society has a monopoly, on the ground that, since Oxford and Cambridge are represented on its Joint Board, they would be competing against themselves if they entered this field. This is obviously a temporary arrangement, for at some future date the work of the London Society will probably be absorbed by the new Teaching University for London. In the meantime, however, it is worth noting that in the neighbourhood of London, but outside the Postal District, the London Society competes with the Universities. Speaking broadly, Oxford and Cambridge are competitors in the remainder of England, though the competition

---

[1] Either directly or through the Hebdomadal Council. A few members are added by the Vice-Chancellor and the Proctors.

is of a limited character. Neither seeks to supplant the other, but both go wherever their services are in request. An increasing number of towns seek a lecturer sometimes from the one, sometimes from the other. An exception, however, exists in those centres which the University of Cambridge has affiliated to itself for a term of three or four years. In parts of the North of England the older Universities find a third competitor in the Victoria University, which has no monopoly, but the natural protection due to its being on the spot. In Durham and Northumberland, Cambridge works in conjunction with the Durham University. There are various opinions on the question of competition. Some people consider that it is detrimental to the standard of work aimed at. Personally, we can quite see the objections to the principle of competition, and think that it should not be unlimited in its scope, but we believe that hitherto it has contributed greatly to the life of the movement, and done little or no harm. It adds *esprit de corps* to the incentives of the lecturer—a factor which we may note plays a great part in the College systems of Oxford and Cambridge.

Each of the four authorities has a staff of lecturers, a few of whom devote themselves wholly to Extension work, but most of them hold some second appointment. Some names appear on the lists of two different staffs, and the London Society makes all the Oxford and Cambridge staffs *ipso facto* members of its own. If, therefore, a London centre desires to do so, it may, through the London office, make an offer of employment to almost any Extension lecturer in England.

Two important steps have been taken during the

past year (1890-91) to strengthen and consolidate the position of the lecturers. The Oxford Delegates and the Cambridge Syndicate have each invited representative lecturers to be present at their meetings, and the lecturers attached to the three branches of the movement—Oxford, Cambridge, and London—have formed a Lecturers' Association, a threefold committee of which watches over the interests of the three groups of lecturers. It is possible that the formation of this association may gradually lead to an arrangement by which every lecturer may freely obtain employment in connection with any one of the three departments of the system.

One of the newest features in the work of the central organisations is the issue of monthly magazines, which have already done much to bind the "centres" to the Universities and to one another. By giving cohesion to the movement, and affording opportunities for the public discussion of policy, they will doubtless be one of the strongest levers in further progress. Oxford led the way in 1889 with a tentative effort—a circular issued from time to time giving the latest arrangements. The object was the modest one of saving a large amount of letter-writing in the office. In February, 1890, the *University Extension Journal* was started in London, under the management of the London Society, and as its official organ. In August of the same year the Oxford Delegates decided to convert their private circular into the *Oxford University Extension Gazette*, which has since appeared regularly. In the meantime, in March, 1890, the South Western Association began the publication of a small quarterly journal of its own, of which only four numbers have as yet been issued.

_{University Extension Journalism.}

It is probably well that the movement should be represented by at least two organs, and that expression should be thus given to the somewhat different views of policy which are often taken by equally keen upholders of the same cause.

The Educational Character of the Work.

Turning now from questions of organisation to the character of the work done in the centres, we have in the first place the following analysis of the subjects of the courses during the last session.

	History and Political Economy.	Literature and Art.	Natural Science.
Oxford	95	33	64
Cambridge	33	32	70
London	31	39	57
	159	104	191

In addition there were three courses on Philosophy given in connection with the London Society.

There is thus a marked preponderance on the "Arts" side in the Oxford work, a slight excess on the same side in the London work, but a small excess on the "Science" side in connection with Cambridge. This condition of things will, however, be wholly altered in the coming session, when the Oxford Delegates alone will have no fewer than sixteen lecturers wholly employed in scientific teaching under the County Councils, and delivering during the winter more than 150 courses of lectures.

Examinations.

Examinations, though they play a very subordinate part in the University Extension system, and are far from being a complete measure either of the efficiency or of the total good it achieves, yet afford the most definite test which can be brought to bear on the attainments of the students. While, therefore, we give below specimen examination papers and extracts from the reports of the examiners, it must be clearly borne in mind that, owing to various causes, many excellent students are prevented from submitting themselves to examination, and that for many reasons it would be most undesirable to lay too much stress on this aspect of the work.

In their report for 1890-91 the Oxford Delegates make the following remarks :—

"During the year the Examiners have prepared general reports on the character of the papers submitted to them in the final examinations, held at the end of most of the courses. The final examination on a course of lectures is never conducted by the Lecturer, but by Examiners appointed by the Delegates, who select, as far as possible, present or former Examiners in the Final Honour Schools of the University. As showing the standard reached by many of the candidates in the final examinations on University Extension Courses, Mr. York Powell, one of the Examiners, wrote : 'The papers classed as "distinguished" would have been accepted in Oxford as distinctly belonging to the honour class : the "pass" standard is that which would be adopted in the Oxford Pass School.' Mr. Lodge reported : 'In awarding distinction I have looked for a standard of knowledge and ability that would do credit to a candidate in the Honour Schools of the University.' Mr. A. H. Johnson wrote : 'Although few of the papers which I have looked over reached the first-class standard, a very considerable proportion of them were fully up to a good second-class standard.' In this connection, it may be pointed out that of the candidates who entered for the final University Extension Examinations during the year, more than one-third received certificates of distinction."

The Council of the London Society speak in a similar strain in their report for 1890 :—

"The examiner of the course on the 'Problems of Poverty' at the Marylebone Centre says : 'Of two of the candidates it can only be said that their papers were astonishingly good, with a completeness and style of expression rarely found. All showed a remarkable interest in the subject of the lectures, and a praiseworthy grasp of detail. In particular, the question on the history of the *Poor Law*, and that on methods of treating pauper *children*, were very thoroughly attempted, the answers in four or five cases being admirable short essays. The fact was continually obtruded on the attention of the examiner that the candidates wrote as if they were discussing practical business and not mere bookwork.' The examiner in 'Electricity' at Crouch End remarks: 'Perhaps the best set of papers which I have ever met with; most of the candidates had evidently thoroughly grasped the subject, and the average number of marks was very high.' In the reports on the examinations in Literary subjects, the examiners speak of the 'high level of average merit,' and the evidences of 'steady reading during the progress of the lectures,' and the Council are satisfied that the educational efficiency of the work is markedly increasing."

The following examination papers, selected from a large number of like character, will convey to those who are not familiar with the standards mentioned in these Oxford reports a clearer idea both of the information and ability expected by the Examiners, and of the general scope of the teaching.

OXFORD UNIVERSITY EXTENSION LECTURES.
THE MAKING OF NATIONS.
[*Not more than* seven *questions to be tried.*]

1. WHAT reasons may be given for the progress of the Aryan races of Europe during the last twenty-four centuries?
2. Show the importance of (1) the Greek Colonies; (2) the Greek Kingdoms in the East.
3. Upon what foundations did the Roman Empire of the West rest?
4. Account for (1) the origin and (2) persistence of the Holy Roman Empire.

5. *a.* "Paris has made France quite as much as France has made Paris."

b. "France, directly and indirectly, has done more good than harm to Germany, and has contributed no little to bring about German Unity."

c. "There are three Germanies: the Protestant, military Germany, which has grown out of Prussia; the Catholic, Austrian Germany, which is so powerful in South-East Europe; and the free, democratic Germany, which we call Switzerland."

Examine these three propositions.

6. Show the chief causes of the rapid spread of Islam over E. Asia and N. Africa.

7. What were the principal effects of the Crusades (1) upon Europe; (2) upon the East?

8. Account for the decay of the Turkish power in the last 150 years.

9. Note the chief steps in the growth of Russia. Upon what bases does her power stand?

10. Why was the Unity of Italy so long delayed? How was it finally accomplished?

11. Show the importance of Spain as a colonial power.

12. How has the transmarine empire of Great Britain come into existence? What causes have made the inhabitants of the United Kingdom successful colonists?

13. Show the importance of (1) language and (2) race in the formation of a nation.

14. Draw sketch maps showing the extent of the (1) Greek Orthodox Church, (2) the Latin races, (3) the non-Aryan races in Europe.

OXFORD UNIVERSITY EXTENSION LECTURES.
PURITAN REVOLUTION.
[*Not more than* six *questions should be tried.*]

1. What were the chief sources from which the Stuart idea of royal prerogative was drawn?

2. Explain the terms Arminianism, Anabaptism, Calvinism; and distinguish the various applications of the word Puritan.

3. In what respect has modern research tended to modify the views held as to the personal conduct (1) of James I., and (2) of George Villiers, Duke of Buckingham?

4. What apparent contradictions are there in the character of Charles I., and how far can they be explained?

5. "That fire, which did shortly burn the whole kingdom, might at that time have been covered under with a bushel." Is this a fair account of the state of English feeling at the opening of the Short Parliament?

6. What were the weak points in the political theories of Eliot and of Strafford respectively?

7. To what extent can the Civil War be called a war of classes?

8. Give a sketch of the military movements in the "Second Civil War."

9. On what grounds can it be said that Charles I. himself brought about his own trial and condemnation?

10. What evidence is there that Cromwell's views underwent change and development as he rose to supreme power?

OXFORD UNIVERSITY EXTENSION LECTURES.
HISTORY AND PRINCIPLES OF ARCHITECTURE.

[*Not more than* six *questions to be tried.*]

1. Explain and illustrate the place of "truth" in Architectural construction.

2. Name the principal orders of Greek Architecture, and describe their leading peculiarities.

3. What traces do we find in various styles of Architecture of an earlier timber construction?

4. Draw a plan of the Parthenon, and show in what particulars it satisfied the religious and artistic requirements of the Athenians.

5. Descibe by plan, or otherwise, a Roman villa, and show why the Roman excelled in domestic, rather than religious Architecture.

6. Explain the following terms:—abacus, acanthus, basilica, entablature, frieze, panel, peristyle.

7. What were the chief differences in the liturgical arrangements of Eastern and Western churches, and their influence on the form and style of building?

8. Under what conditions did the imitation of natural objects find a place in Architectural construction and ornamentation?

9. What were the chief features of early Syrian Architecture? How far did these depend upon local conditions? Estimate the influence of this style upon mediæval Architecture.

OXFORD UNIVERSITY EXTENSION LECTURES.
GEOLOGY.
[Not more than six questions to be tried.]

1. State what is known about the temperature and density of the interior of the earth, and indicate shortly how our knowledge of these matters is arrived at.

2. Describe and give rough sketches of what is seen by the aid of the microscope in thin sections of granite and pitchstone. What was it that caused each rock to have its distinguishing character?

3. In what way is pumice formed? If a bit of pumice and a bag full of powdered pumice were thrown into water, what would happen to the two? Explain why.

4. Draw a section showing an arrangement of strata which will tend to cause springs on a hillside, and distinguish between those cases where springs seldom fail, and those where they cease to run after a spell of dry weather.

5. Explain the way in which coal, and the rocks among which it is found were formed, stating the facts on which your explanation is based.

6. State the physical conditions necessary for the formation of glaciers. Beginning with the source from whence it is derived, follow water through all the stages it passes through till a glacier results, and show how in the end it may get back to where it first came from.

7. Give the distinctive characters of deposits formed in the sea far from land, in the sea near the shore, in fresh-water lakes, and at the mouths of rivers.

8. Draw a section showing two groups of rocks separated by an unconformity and faults, some of which were formed before and some after the deposition of the upper group.

9. Enumerate the main points of difference between Palæolithic and Neolithic man. How would you account for these differences?

OXFORD UNIVERSITY EXTENSION LECTURES, ARRANGED BY THE DEVON COUNTY COUNCIL.

MAY 11TH, 1891.

EXAMINATION IN CHEMISTRY.

[*Not more than* seven *questions to be answered.*]

1. Draw a candle flame and describe its parts. What becomes of the candle as it burns away?
2. What makes air impure when too many persons are in a room? Why is ventilation wanted? How could you test the air in a well?
3. Describe the chief differences between sea water, spring water, rain water. How is distilled water made?
4. What causes water to be hard? How can hard water be made soft?
5. Explain the use of a Davy lamp. What is paraffin oil? Why are some oils dangerous or likely to be explosive?
6. Name some different kinds of manure. What substances do they yield to the growing plants?
7. How is lime made from limestone? Mention some differences between limestone and lime.
8. Give the composition of oil of vitriol, salt, bones. What are their uses on a farm?
9. What is the principal source of ammonia? Describe some of the leading properties of this substance. Explain the action of lime with manure containing ammonia.
10. What substances do plants take from the air? Do such substances ever return to the air? Explain how.
11. How should a clay land be drained? Explain what effects on plants and land are produced by drainage.
12. What are oxygen and nitrogen: how are they found in nature: how are they prepared pure? Give a short account of their properties.

The Various Classes of Students. It is an especial characteristic of the University Extension system that, with slight variations, it is applicable to the wants of nearly all classes of the community. In the case of afternoon lectures, probably 70 per cent. of the audiences are ladies of leisure and older school-girls. University Extension has indeed played a great part in the movement for the higher education of women, the vast majority of whom are tied to their homes, and, though they may possess what are called the "accomplishments," have had very few opportunities of acquiring some of the broader culture on which generous and tolerant views of life are based. We have, personally, been told several times by shrewd observers, of a change for the better in the conversation and social tone of some suburb of a manufacturing town as the result of the delivery of courses of Extension lectures.

A few courses are delivered at local colleges and other fixed seats of learning. Cambridge Extension Lecturers do much of the work at University College, Nottingham, and the London Society gives lectures at the Birkbeck Institute and Gresham College; but the great majority of courses are delivered in the evening to audiences composed, in the main, of the professional classes, of tradesmen and their families, and of artisans. There are several large centres, especially in the north of England, where the local organisation is carried on by Co-operative Societies, and where the audiences, often numbering 400 or 500, are wholly composed of working-men. It is impossible to refer to this important branch of the movement without mentioning the name of the Oxford staff-lecturer, the Rev. W. Hudson Shaw.

Lastly, there must be mentioned the very important class of elementary school teachers, who have availed themselves very largely of the opportunities brought within their reach by the system. Since many of the effects filter through them to the next generation, their attendance is generally felt to be of the utmost importance, and it has become a frequent practice to allow them tickets at reduced prices. At a course delivered by one of the writers at Manchester, some two or three years ago, out of a total average attendance of 400, no fewer than 105 were elementary teachers.

We have spoken of various classes attending the lectures; we must add that audiences wholly of one class are rare. One of the most conspicuous and gratifying characteristics of Extension work is the way in which it brings together students of very different ranks. "In an examination recently held at a lecture-centre, among those to whom were awarded certificates of distinction were a national school-mistress, a young lawyer, a plumber, and a railway signalman."[1] An even more striking instance is mentioned by Dr. Roberts in his recent book, "Eighteen Years of University Extension." At the examination held at the close of a Tyneside course of "Political Economy," attended in part by miners, "the highest place was taken by one of these miners, and the second place by a lady, the daughter of a wealthy manufacturer, the member of Parliament for the borough."

Sequence of Subjects. University Extension arose in the first instance as a protest against the single-lecture system of the Mechanics' Institutes. Its special characteristic was to be the sequence of *lectures* on the same subject, or the "course" of lectures. We are now moving a step forwards, and the constant effort of all the University Extension authorities is to induce the centres, where their financial position

[1] Oxford Report, 1889-90.

will admit of it, to arrange the subjects of the successive *courses* in educational sequence. It is clear, however, that the offer of a sequence of courses confined to historical or literary subjects, however admirably arranged to cover a period of three years, will always be likely to estrange the interest of the large minority, to be found in any mixed body of students, who prefer instruction in natural science. Similarly, a "sequence" confined to natural science would alienate the support of many who prefer instruction in history or literature. But, under existing conditions, the financial support of both of these sections of students is necessary to the well-being of an ordinary Extension centre. For this reason we believe that any elaborate sequence of courses will ordinarily be found impracticable until funds are forthcoming, from public or private sources, on such a scale as to allow of parallel courses on different subjects being delivered during the same session. The various tastes and needs of the students will then be met, while, at the same time, each student will be encouraged to single out one or more subjects for special study. But it is in the highest degree improbable that such parallel "sequences" can, under the ordinary conditions prevailing in this country, be self-supporting; and it is for this reason chiefly that we urge the expediency of State aid.

Sequence of studies and permanence of local organisation are the two objects which the old Universities desire to encourage under their Affiliation Statutes. In 1886 a statute of the University of Cambridge was approved by the Queen in Council, giving to the University the power of affiliating to

<small>Affiliation of Local Centres to Oxford and Cambridge.</small>

itself any Local Lecture Centre which fulfilled certain conditions. The most important privilege obtained by the students of an affiliated centre is the remission, on certain conditions, of one out of the three years of residence at Cambridge necessary for a degree. The centres which have so far availed themselves of the statute, and have undertaken a systematic course of lectures on science and literature, extending over a period of four years, are Hull, Scarborough, Newcastle-on-Tyne, Sunderland, Derby, Exeter, and Plymouth.

Affiliation under the Oxford Statute only possible to Centres with a permanent Organisation.

Oxford has not as yet affiliated any University Extension Centre; but in 1880 a statute was passed authorising the affiliation to that University of "any College or *Institution* . . . in any part of the British Dominions, . . . in which the majority of the students are of the age of seventeen at least, . . . on the conditions . . . that provision shall have been made for its establishment on a permanent and efficient footing, . . . [and] that it shall allow the University to be represented on its Governing Body, and to take such part in its Examinations as shall from time to time be determined by or under the authority of the University." It is further provided " that the connection between the University and an affiliated College shall be terminable either by a vote of [the] Convocation [of the University], or by a resolution of the Governing Body of the College." It is also arranged that the same Delegacy, which at present controls the Local Examinations, the Examination of Women, and the University Extension System, shall have authority in matters concerning the affiliated Colleges. The same privilege of a year's remission of residence is granted by this statute as by the Cambridge Affiliation Statute.[1] The local colleges which have as yet affiliated themselves to Oxford are Lampeter, Nottingham, and Sheffield. It is clear, however, that under the terms of the Oxford Statute any University Extension centre, which desires to ask Convocation to affiliate it to the University of Oxford, must have previously established itself on a much more permanent basis than has been hitherto contemplated as necessary by the local organisers.

It is very necessary, however, that there should be no misconceptions as to the meaning and probable effects of these statutes. The vast majority of University Extension students are already pledged to a career in life, and to them two years of residence are just as prohibitory as three. Moreover, the privileges of affiliation are only granted under the Cambridge, as well as under the Oxford, Statute to such students of affiliated centres or colleges as have passed an examination in Euclid, Algebra, Arithmetic, and two Languages, one of them being Latin, and, at Oxford, the second being Greek. There is the further proviso, of very little importance, however, to the better class of University Extension students, that such privileges shall only belong to those who subsequently pass an Honours Examination in the University.

We do not think that the special privileges of affiliation will be *directly* useful to any very large proportion of University Extension students. The aim of the great majority of these students is not to make themselves professional scholars, but by self-culture to widen and deepen their ideals of life. In our judgment, the true interests of education

[1] *See* "Statutes of the University of Oxford," Ed. 1889, pp. 6-8.

make it in the highest degree undesirable to grant
any privileges which would lower the value of a
University degree. Nor would it be wise to encourage any large number of persons *of merely
average ability* to sacrifice suitable means of livelihood in order to reside in the University for the
purpose of graduating as B.A. The labour market
is already overstocked with graduates of ordinary
attainments. While furnishing men and women, of
all ranks and ages, with stimulus and guidance in
elevating studies, University Extension must not
seek to inspire unsuitable persons with an ambition
for callings for which they are not intellectually
fitted. The hope of many of those who are engaged in the "extra-mural" work of Oxford and
Cambridge is, that the Universities may gradually see
their way to confine more closely their *internal* organisation, apart from vacation courses, to the function of research and to the more exclusive instruction
of advanced scholars and teachers, while at the same
time controlling and inspiring a vast external system
of higher general education, the ramifications of
which may eventually extend to every corner of the
land. The local centres of such an external system will have to act as roots, sucking out of every
class in the nation all who have special gifts for
teaching, scholarship, or research, and passing them
on to the resident teachers in the University for
higher training. Apart from the *status* which formal affiliation to the Universities will confer on the
best Extension centres, the affiliation scheme will
be chiefly useful in discovering and helping forward
specially gifted students who would otherwise fail
to obtain the advantages and discipline of University life. In Mr. Ruskin's words, "We must

leave no Giotto among the hill shepherds." The University Extension scheme enables us to discover great ability; affiliation makes it possible to provide such ability with its easiest means of complete development.

We may here, perhaps, refer to the scheme of "Home Reading Circles," started some years ago as an effort at sequence of studies, though not always connected with lectures. Home Reading Circles.

The idea was that isolated students in small places out of reach of an Extension centre, and Extension students in the off-season, should join a circle to read books on some definite subject under the leadership of an expert. The members sent periodical essays to the leader of the circle. The scheme had the advantage of reaching the isolated units in the villages. It seemed a promising new development. An elaborate apparatus was contrived, a system of adhesive stamps for the prepayment of the fees on essays came from the Oxford Office, but somehow the idea hung fire.[1] It may be that to some extent the summer courses now being developed leave little room for it. It seems more probable, however, that it lacks the essential element of success. Systematic study generally requires the stimulus and corrective of living touch with the teacher. It is only fair to say, however, that an independent organisation, the National Home Reading Union, after a period of comparative failure, has now 7,000 members. Its aim is not to compete with University Extension, but rather to reach the boys and girls who are leaving the elementary schools, and to prepare them to profit by Extension Lectures. We welcome its help with great pleasure, though

[1] *See* Oxford Report, 1890.

we doubt whether, in the event of University Extension Lectures being made cheaper and the centres far more numerous, any scheme for associated study would succeed which did not include, as a chief element, personal intercourse with a teacher.

Summer Meetings.

The Summer Meetings are certainly one of the most striking of all the recent developments of the system. The history of their origin has already been stated, and here we have merely to describe their organisation, and to point out their place in the general scheme of University Extension. The first Summer Meeting was held at Oxford in August, 1888,[1] and was attended by 900 students. Financial reasons made it necessary to limit its duration to ten days. Short courses of from three to six lectures were delivered in the mornings, while the evenings were devoted to addresses by eminent men on literary and scientific subjects The opportunity was taken of holding conferences of the local secretaries and other organisers who happened to be present, and there can be no question but that the movement greatly benefited by the ideas then struck out. The foundation of many new centres was directly traceable to the enthusiasm of this meeting. It was thrown impartially open alike to Oxford, Cambridge and London students.

Oxford, 1888.

The first experiment having succeeded—it being proved that, if invited, the students would come to the University—the next point was to keep them in residence for a longer time. The second meeting in August, 1889, was announced to consist of two " parts,"[2] of which Part I. was in all essen-

Oxford, 1889.

---

[1] Report of Oxford Summer Meeting, 1888.
[2] *Ibid.*, 1889.

tial respects to resemble the meeting of 1888. Part II. was to be open to those students who could afford to remain on for an additional period of three weeks, to be devoted to quiet study. One thousand students came to Part I., no fewer than 150 remained on for Part II. On all hands it was admitted that both parts were successful. As with the winter courses in the centres, so with the Summer Meeting at Oxford, many different classes of people with their different wants had to be kept in view. Several hundred of the students were teachers, who came for new ideas and methods which should throw a new life into their teaching. As in the earlier year, many new centres derived their impulse from Part I. We have, therefore, facts, as well as opinions, tending to show that the work then begun was, in not a few cases, continued with perseverance.

In 1890 a third meeting took place, with arrangements similar to those of the previous year, but, for various reasons, with somewhat less success. With the fourth meeting, however, held in the present year, progress has been resumed, and numerically, financially, and educationally, the 1891 gathering has shown a distinct advance on the best of its three predecessors. This is the more striking, because the programme advertised and carried through exhibits a more strenuous and less disguised effort at sequence of subjects than, so far as we are aware, has ever yet been attempted in connection with University Extension. Under these circumstances we venture to summarise the sequences of courses then delivered: the high-water mark of actual achievements, as opposed to mere ideals. *Oxford, 1890.* *Oxford, 1891.*

OXFORD SUMMER MEETING, 1891.

COURSES OF LECTURES AND CLASSES.

A.—Sequence of Seventy-two Lectures and Classes on Mediæval History, Literature, Architecture, and Economics.

[This Sequence will be continued by similar Sequences at the Meetings of 1892, 1893, and 1894. The Subject of the corresponding Sequence of Lectures in 1892 will be *The Renaissance and the Reformation;* in 1893 *The Seventeenth Century;* and in 1894 *The Eighteenth Century.*]

Subject.	No. in Course.	Lecturer.
Introductory Lecture—A Short Survey of the Thirteenth Century	One	Frederic Harrison, M.A., late Fellow of Wadham College.
Some Authorities on Mediæval History	Three	F. York Powell, M.A., Student and Tutor of Christ Church; Examiner to the Oxford University Extension.
The Frank Empire	Three	H. J. Mackinder, M.A., Reader in Geography in the University of Oxford; Oxford University Extension Staff-Lecturer.
The Norman Conquest	Three	Rev. A. H. Johnson, M.A., Lecturer at University, Balliol, Merton, Trinity, and Hertford Colleges; Examiner to the Oxford University Extension.
Mediæval Venice	Three	Rev. W. Hudson Shaw, M.A., Fellow of Balliol College; Oxford University Extension Staff-Lecturer.
The Mediæval Town, as illustrated by Mediæval Oxford	One	C. B. Mallet, M.A., Balliol College; Oxford University Extension Staff-Lecturer.
The Early History of Parliament	Three	A. Lionel Smith, M.A., Fellow and Tutor of Balliol College; Examiner to the Oxford University Extension.
The Constitutional History of England (Class for Study)	Twelve	G. Noel Richardson, M.A., Lecturer in History at Oriel College; Examiner to the Oxford University Extension.
Church and State in Mediæval England: (i.) The Church and the Making of England: Theodore of Tarsus (ii.) The Church and the Crown: Anselm and Becket (iii.) The Church and the Great Charter: Stephen Langton (iv.) The English Church and the Papacy: Edward I. and Boniface VIII.	Four	J. A. R. Marriott, M.A., Lecturer at Worcester College; Lecturer to the Non-Collegiate Delegacy and to the Association for the Education of Women in Oxford; Oxford University Extension Staff-Lecturer.

Subject.	No. in Course.	Lecturer.
The Monasteries	One	A. G. Little, B.A., Balliol College; Oxford University Extension Lecturer.
Mediæval Romance and the "Morte d'Arthur"	One	F. S. Boas, M.A., late Exhibitioner of Balliol College; University Oxford Extension Staff-Lecturer.
The Mediæval Drama	One	F. S. Boas, M.A.
Chaucer	Three	J. Churton Collins, M.A., Balliol College; Oxford University Extension Staff-Lecturer.
Dante	Three	Rev. P. Wicksteed, M.A., Warden of University Hall, London; London University Extension Lecturer.
Dante (Class for Study)	Twelve	F. York Powell, M.A.
Mediæval Allegory	Six	R. G. Moulton, M.A., Christ's College, Cambridge; Cambridge University Extension Lecturer.
A Mediæval Art Student: His Life and Training	One	W. G. Collingwood, M.A., late Scholar of University College; Hon. President of the Ruskin Reading Guild; Oxford University Extension Lecturer.
Mediæval Architecture (illustrated)	One	Rev. G. H. West, D.D., F.G.S., A.R.I.B.A., late Junior Student of Christ Church; Oxford University Extension Lecturer.
Gothic Architecture (with illustrative excursions)	Three	Rev. F. H. Woods, B.D., late Fellow and Tutor of St. John's College; Warburtonian Lecturer at Lincoln's Inn.
The Mediæval Land System	One	Rev. A. H. Johnson, M.A.
Contrast between Mediæval and Modern Ideas on— (i.) Investment of Money (ii.) Position of the Workman (iii.) Duties of the State	One	M. E. Sadler, M.A., Student and Steward of Christ Church; Secretary to the Oxford University Extension.
Master and Man in the Middle Ages	Three	M. E. Sadler, M.A.
The Craft Guild	One	J. A. Hobson, M.A., Lincoln College; Oxford University Extension Lecturer.
Work and Wages in the Fourteenth Century	One	E. L. S. Horsburgh, B.A., late Exhibitioner of Queen's College; Oxford University Extension Lecturer.

B.—Sequence of Thirty-three Lectures and Classes on Greek History, Literature and Art.

[To be continued in 1892 and 1893. The Sequence in 1892 will deal with Thucydides and the Greek Tragedians.]

Subject.	No. in Course.	Lecturer.
Homer.	Two	Arthur Sidgwick, M.A., Fellow and Tutor of Corpus Christi College.
Homeric Archæology (illustrated)	One	Percy Gardner, M.A., Lincoln College; Lincoln and Merton Professor of Archæology and Art in the University of Oxford.
Homer's "Odyssey;" (Class for the Study of Books VI. and IX.)	Twelve	E. K. Chambers, B.A., late Scholar of Corpus Christi College; Lecturer to the Association for the Education of Women in Oxford; Oxford University Extension Lecturer.
The Persian Wars	Three	R. W. Macan, M.A., Fellow and Tutor of University College; Reader in Ancient History in the University of Oxford.
Herodotus (Class for the Study of Books V.-IX.)	Twelve	F. C. Montague, M.A., late Fellow of Oriel College.
The Parthenon (illustrated with lantern slides)	Three	Miss Jane Harrison, Newnham College, Cambridge; Oxford University Extension Lecturer.

C.—Sequence of Twenty Lectures and Classes on Geology.

Subject.	No. in Course.	Lecturer.
Geology	One	A. H. Green, M.A., F.R.S., late Fellow of Gonville and Caius College, Cambridge; Professor of Geology in the University of Oxford.
A Course of Practical Lessons in Geological Map-Making (with excursions)	Twelve	Professor Green.
Geology	One	A. B. Badger, B.A., late Open Exhibitioner of New College; Lecturer on Palæontology for the Professor of Geology; Associate of the Mason Science College, Birmingham; Oxford University Extension Lecturer.
A Course of Practical Geology (with excursions in the neighbourhood)	Five	A. B. Badger, B.A.
Geology	One	C. Carus-Wilson, F.G.S., F.R.G.S., late of the Royal School of Mines; formerly Lecturer on Geology at Wargrave Military College; Oxford University Extension Lecturer.

D. — Sequence of Twenty-one Lectures and Classes on Chemistry.

Subject.	No. in Course.	Lecturer.
Chemistry . . .	One	V. Perronet Sells, M.A., F.C.S., late Open Exhibitioner of New College ; Oxford University Extension Lecturer.
Class in Practical Chemistry	Eighteen	J. E Marsh, B.A., Demonstrator in Chemistry at the University Museum, Oxford.
The Benzene Ring .	Two	W. Odling, M.A., F.R.S., Fellow of Worcester College ; Waynflete Professor of Chemistry in the University of Oxford.

In addition to these sequences there were more than thirty lectures on other topics, including three on Heredity, by Mr. Poulton, F.R.S. ; three on the Kindergarten system, by Miss Walenn; and six practical classes in Astronomy, conducted by Mr. Plummer; besides single lectures by Dr. Bailey, Mr. Keene, and others. A guide to the choice of books for courses of reading preparatory to the meeting was issued six months beforehand.

About 1,100 students were in residence at Oxford from July 31 to August 11, inclusive, of whom more than 250 took supplementary tickets entitling them to attend until August 16, and about 160 remained for the final period, from August 16 to September 1.

In 1890 and 1891 Cambridge followed the example set by Oxford by holding "courses of study in Cambridge" during the month of August. Owing to the circumstances that many Undergraduates reside at Cambridge during the long vacation, and that Cambridge has not a splendid group of halls as fitted for the purpose as the Oxford Examination Schools, the sister University has not

Cambridge, 1890 and 1891.

yet undertaken a great meeting similar to the First Part of the Oxford gathering. Forty-one students, however—nine men and thirty-two women—assembled in 1890, and a somewhat similar number in 1891, and availed themselves of the opportunities offered by the University laboratories, museums, and art galleries. In the former year the principle upon which the Syndicate acted was not to offer any instruction which could, with equal advantage, be given in a local Centre. In the latter, however, they determined to add courses of lectures on History and Literature to their programme, which had previously included only Natural Science and Art. The idea of such a Summer Meeting has been very contagious. The National Home Reading Union held gatherings at Blackpool in 1889, 1890, and 1891, and Edinburgh, it may be mentioned, has tried to acclimatise the scheme in Scotland. But, obviously, no place has the same available wealth of educational appliances that are to be found idle and ready to hand at Oxford in the months of July and August.

Scholarships.

There is one feature in connection with these meetings which is, as yet, little developed, but which has great significance. Ten days at Oxford, even when the lodgings are put on tariff, together with the travelling to and from the University, imply an expenditure of about £5, the whole month one of £10.[1] To poorer Extension students these are prohibitive sums. After the first meeting,[2] several subscribers came forward with the

[1] Oxford Summer Meeting Programme, 1890.
[2] The first four Scholarships were given by Mr. J. G. Talbot, M.P., the Marquis of Ripon, K.G., and Mr. F. D. Mocatta. Mr. Talbot, addressing the University Extension Conference, held in Oxford in April, 1887 (the year before the first Summer

offer of scholarships for poor students tenable at the second meeting. These scholarships were given to Oxford Extension students who had qualified by attending certain courses of lectures in the centres in the winter. They were awarded on the results of a competition of essays, among others to two carpenters, two clerks, a fustian weaver, a dockyard artisan, and three elementary teachers.[1] In 1890 the number of the scholarships, by the kindness of the previous other donors, was increased, and there were present in Oxford in that year more than twenty comparatively poor people holding scholarships of £5 or £10. Of these at least six were working-men, and at least four elementary teachers.[2] These numbers do not include scholarships tenable at the Oxford and Cambridge meetings which were given to London students.

The report of the Examiners who awarded the Oxford scholarships in 1890, indicating as it does the standard of excellence reached by many of the students of the Extension, is worth producing *in extenso* :[3]—

"There has been a great increase in the number of essays sent in, and the high level reached in the competition last year has been fully maintained.

"The historical and other essays written by working-men are worthy of special praise.

"In science, the number of good and deserving essays was

Meeting was held), offered a scholarship "to be devoted to the maintaining of a student who can come to Oxford during the summer months and obtain such advantages as Oxford is able to afford."

[1] Oxford Extension Report, 1890.
[2] Oxford Official Circular for University Extension, 1890.
[3] *Ibid.*

far in advance of anything experienced in previous years. The best essays were extremely good, and proved that very hard and conscientious work had been done. The majority of the essays were up to Scholarship standard.

"The best essay written on the literary subject showed a remarkable amount of reading and thought, but the Examiners regret that more essays were not written on the subjects drawn from English Literature.

"J. FRANCK BRIGHT.
(*Master of University College.*)
"A. SIDGWICK.
(*Fellow and Tutor of Corpus Christi College.*)
"L. R. PHELPS.
(*Fellow and Tutor of Oriel College.*)
"E. B. POULTON.
(*F.R.S., Late Lecturer at Keble and Jesus Colleges.*)"

The results of Scholarship Competition for 1891 are thus referred to in the last Oxford Report:—

"The prize essays submitted to the Delegates in the competition for Scholarships tenable at the Summer Meeting have again reached a high level of excellence, and the number of competitors has largely increased. The competition is limited to those who have attended Oxford University Extension courses during the year, and the success of the efforts of the lecturers to interest men and women of all ranks of life in systematic study is shown by the fact that among the competitors for the Scholarships were cotton-weavers, brushmakers, printers, bookbinders, mechanical engineers, and other artisans. The competition for the Scholarships offered to Elementary Teachers also produced, as in former years, a number of excellent essays."

The following was the list from which the competitors had to select the subjects of their essays in the present year. It was published in the March number of the *Oxford University Extension Gazette*, and the scholarships, to the value of £130, were awarded in the following June.

SUBJECTS.

(1) *History* (one only to be selected).

(i.) The development of English energy and power in the sixteenth century.

(ii.) The results of the Puritan Revolution.

(iii.) The influence of England on Europe since the accession of the House of Hanover.

(2) *Literature* (one only to be selected).

(i.) Distinguish, with full illustrations, the various kinds of comedy.

(ii.) Discuss and illustrate the principal points in which Shakespeare's dramatic writings show originality.

(iii.) Show in the case of any of the great writers of this century the relation between literature and the needs and ideas of the day.

(iv.) What is the use of Poetry?

(3) *Political Economy.*

What means of improving the condition of the working class are suggested by a study of the past?

(4) *Science* (one only to be selected).

(i.) Heat.   (ii.) The Atomic Theory.

(iii.) Discuss the permanence of the great ocean basins.

In addition to the Scholarships awarded by the Delegates, which are open to University Extension students from any Oxford centre, there are local Scholarships also tenable at the Summer Meeting, but given by local committees or by individuals to students from particular centres or districts. And in this connection we have to mention the admirable example which is being set by Mr. T. D. Galpin of Roehampton, who is offering to the Dorset County Council a considerable sum of money, the interest of which is to supply annual Scholarships tenable at the Oxford or Cambridge meetings by natives of, or *bona fide* residents in, the

County of Dorset. The Union of Working Men's Co-operative Societies provided six small Scholarships to enable students, who had been most successful in certain educational classes arranged by the Union, to attend the Oxford Summer Meeting of 1891;[1] while the Oxford City Council, out of the funds at its disposal for the purpose of technical education, gave similar Scholarships to enable four Oxford working-men to attend the scientific classes at the same meeting.

The Necessity of "Missionary" Work.

Everything thus seems to show that the standard of the work done by University Extension students is rising steadily year by year. It is important, however, to remember that we must not rest content with this kind of progress alone. Great as may appear the average number of students now in attendance at the classes, we have as yet only touched the fringe of the problem of the higher education of the masses, and, while the better centres constantly approximate to a University standard of work, the missionary side of the movement must not be allowed to flag. The country villages, in some ways the finest of all the missionary fields open to us, are as yet practically untouched. In London the University Extension Society attributes much of its recent growth to the success of the People's Lecture Scheme in interesting new bodies of students. But the most striking illustration of the value of what is really the "thin edge of the wedge" method, is to be seen in the wonderfully rapid growth of the Oxford Extension. Though the controversy which was centred round the Oxford short courses

Long and Short Courses.

[1] Six similar Scholarships are again offered by the Co-operative Union for 1892.

is now in the main settled, it has involved questions of policy of such vital importance to the future of the movement, that it cannot be passed over in silence. The large majority of the Oxford courses still consist of six lectures, while those of the London Society are mostly of ten, and those of Cambridge, eleven or twelve.[1] Cambridge and London refuse to give "certificates" for examinations on courses of less than ten, eleven, or twelve lectures. Oxford, until 1890, gave them on courses of not less than six.[2] It was felt by some of those who were chiefly interested in the Cambridge and London work that the Oxford policy was dangerous. It might depreciate the value of the certificate, which had hitherto been associated with the idea of the full course of twelve lectures. Some centres might be led to save themselves the trouble of collecting the necessary funds for twelve lectures, if they were given the opportunity of taking only six instead.

The contention of Oxford, on the other hand, was that a very large number of small towns, and the poorer districts of many large ones, were prevented from adopting University Extension by the considerable expense involved in a course of twelve lectures; that working-men's societies, especially, felt the outlay required for twelve lectures beyond the means at their disposal. It was pointed out that it was particularly desirable that University Extension should spread exactly in those places and among those classes to which experience had shown the cost of twelve lectures to be often

[1] Oxford and Cambridge Reports for 1889-90; London Report for 1889.
[2] Cf. Oxford, Cambridge, and London Regulations.

prohibitive. There were also a number of towns in which University Extension teaching had been suspended. In some of these its original promoters had suffered from a deficit. It was extremely desirable to get these towns to try again. "Only let these small towns and poorer districts begin on a modest scale," it was argued, "and you will find them ready to venture on the work, or to renew their connection with it. The local committees consist of men and women who are sincerely interested in education; you may trust them not to rest content with an incomplete course as soon as they can afford a complete one. Financial reasons, not want of educational interest, hold them back. Many of them, too, are not well off, and are unable to afford the risk of a heavy outlay. Above all, they may be trusted not to deal with the two Universities as between rival shopkeepers. They will be loyal to the University with which they have been so long connected. While they would no doubt gladly avail themselves of freedom to employ indifferently Oxford and Cambridge lecturers, no local committee would, in a spirit of mere commercial competition, transfer its allegiance to the cheapest market."

To this it was subsequently replied that there was no harm in offering six lectures to towns which could not afford twelve. But it was contended that, if a town took only half a course, it should be debarred from having an examination on it. The full privileges should be reserved for those who availed themselves of the full system. If a town could have an examination and certificates on six lectures, there would be no incentive for it to make a further effort to have twelve.

Those who believed in the Oxford system still held their ground. The object of University Extension, they pointed out, was to provide *systematic* teaching for adults. Unless the students attending the lectures were encouraged to look forward to an examination at the end of the course, their attendance might become irregular; they might become slack in writing weekly exercises; the quality of their work might deteriorate. Besides, it was expedient to show those towns which could not arrange the full course of twelve lectures, what the University Extension method really was. This would not be done by merely showing them part of it. It was necessary to maintain the complete educational system of University Extension wherever it was established.

Such were the two sides of the question in debate. Happily the controversy is now at an end. It has been found that by the short course system a large number of new centres have been founded, but that this increase in the Oxford work has not been made at the expense of either the Cambridge or London systems, both of which have also continued to grow. Firstly, by the arrangement of courses at fortnightly instead of weekly intervals; secondly, as their means permitted, by the increase in the number of lectures, the Oxford centres have steadily lengthened the period of study covered by the course. Three or four years ago Oxford gave only one or two courses of twelve lectures; in the session 1890-91, however, the statistics published, show that there were

124 courses of 6 lectures;
  8   ,,   7   ,,
  7   ,,   8   ,,

                1 course of   9 lectures ;
                4 courses of 10   ,,
                2   ,,   11   ,,
            and 47   ,,   12   ,,

And in a similar way the period of study available for guided reading in connection with the lectures has increased from an average of eight and a half weeks in 1887-88 to twelve and a half weeks in 1890-91.[1] In 1890, however, a modification was made in the Oxford regulations, which met with the approval of all parties. The Oxford certificate is now awarded only after courses of twelve lectures : examination is permitted, as before, on all courses of six lectures and upwards; the standard of examination is maintained at the same level, irrespective of the number of lectures in the course; but students who are successful in examination on the shorter courses receive, in lieu of a certificate, a printed statement of the examiner's award.

Statistics.   In the session 1890-91,[2] 192 courses of lectures were delivered in connection with Oxford, 135 in connection with Cambridge, 130 in connection with London. Since during the three years 1887-90 the Victoria University had twenty-one courses under its management, we may safely add to our numbers for the session 1890-91 seven courses. This gives us a total of 464 courses. The average number of lectures in a course has been, for Oxford nearly eight, for London about ten, and for Cambridge between eleven and twelve. We may therefore roughly assume an average all round of nine and a half. We have thus a total of 4,408

[1] Oxford Report, 1891.
[2] The following Reports are referred to in this section :—Oxford, session 1890-91 ; Cambridge, session 1890-91 ; London, 1890 ; Victoria, Report for 1887-90.

lectures in one session, and this without counting more than 100 in the Oxford Summer Meeting.

In the same session 20,148 persons attended the Oxford courses, 10,947 the Cambridge courses, 12,923 the London courses. In three years the Victoria courses were attended by about 2,730, giving us a yearly average of 910 to be reckoned to the total for 1890-91. Irrespective of 1,100 members of the Oxford Summer Meeting, we have, therefore, a grand total of 45,028 attendants at the courses in one session. The word "course" has been used rather than lectures to indicate the meaning of these figures. The attendance at each lecture is noted. The average attendance at each lecture of a course can thus be found, and the averages of all the courses, added together, give the above numbers. It should be observed that the statistics of the different authorities are not collected on quite the same principles. The London Society gives "entries for courses" instead of "average attendances," but this probably vitiates the figures only very slightly.

The total number of students examined is not attainable. In the case of Cambridge it is returned at 1,547 for the last session, in that of Oxford, at 1,388. Only Oxford and London publish the number of certificates or "printed statements" awarded: 1,349 students obtained certificates in London; 1,181 passed the examination in connection with Oxford. We shall therefore be well within the mark if we say that 4,300 or nearly ten per cent. of the audiences were examined. If we bear in mind the facts that the audiences are largely composed of adults, and that the certificate has a direct use only for a few people, this is not an unsatisfactory result. In all cases, many of the best students refuse to submit themselves to examination, and we must allow that examination is not the chief end in view in University Extension—only a very valuable method of inciting to thoroughness of work.

The number of lecturers actually employed in the session 1890-91 was in London 37, by the Oxford scheme 33, by the Cambridge scheme 30. Since six of those who lectured in London also lectured in the country for Cambridge, and five also for Oxford, and since one lecturer was on both the Oxford and the Cambridge lists, the total number of lecturers employed was 88. On an average they delivered just under 50 lectures each, without counting Victoria, for which we have no returns under this head.

The number of towns in which the lectures were delivered cannot be accurately stated owing to the difficulty of separating suburbs from their cities. The accompanying maps will, however, give a very fair idea of the distribution of the work. The first shows the towns in which Oxford lectures were delivered in the session 1890-91. The second is a similar map for Cambridge. It should be remembered that at present, owing to various circumstances—mainly financial difficulties—some centres are intermittent, and for this reason some names are absent from the maps in this particular year, though in another they might have appeared. Broadly speaking, Oxford and Cambridge predominate respectively on their two sides of the country. The exceptions are due to various causes, the chief being the personal connection of some prime mover in a neighbourhood with one or other

OXFORD CENTRES, 1890-91.

CAMBRIDGE CENTRES, 1890-91.

University; and, secondly, the occasional failure of a lecturer, a discouragement from time to time encountered by both schemes, and sometimes leading to a transfer of allegiance to the sister University.

A complete statement of the financial condition of the movement cannot be given for lack of published materials. The following facts may, however, be of service:— Finance.

During the five years 1885-90 local committees expended on Oxford courses (exclusive of local expenses) £13,238, and of this amount £7,760 was spent during the two years 1888-90.[1] If we estimate the local expenses at £10 a course, which, on the average, cannot be far from the mark, then in the five years in question we have a local expenditure of about £4,530 on 453 courses. In addition the University granted during the same period for office expenses sums amounting to £1,700, besides an office rent-free.[2] The Oxford Reports state that the Clarendon Press has also rendered substantial assistance in the printing of syllabuses. A great number of books were presented by publishers and others when the Travelling Libraries were first started. These were the chief items of income in the Oxford accounts for five years.

Judging by the statistics of lectures, the total cost of the Oxford system under all the above heads during the year 1890-91 may, perhaps, be set down at about £8,000.

---

[1] Compare Oxford Official Circular on University Extension, 1890.

[2] Oxford University Extension Accounts; presented to the University, 1885—1889.

The published balance-sheet of the London Society for 1890 shows an income of more than £4,500, including more than £1,100 by subscriptions, and an expenditure at least as large as its income. The local expenses are in London rather less than in the country, owing to the smallness of the item for the travelling of the lecturer. If we put them at £8 a course we shall have to add for local expenses say £1,050, making the total annual cost of the London scheme say, £5,600.

We have no figures accessible for Cambridge, but, as the Cambridge courses are on the average longer than those of Oxford, we may perhaps set down the annual cost at £8,000, or the same as Oxford.

Let us add, say, £550 for the Victoria University.

Thus our rough estimate of the present annual cost of University Extension stands thus:—

Oxford	...	£8,000
Cambridge	...	8,000
London	...	5,600
Victoria	...	250
Total		£21,850

or just less than ten shillings a head on the total average attendance.[1] If we put the average number of lectures in a course at nine and a half, we have a cost of about a shilling a lecture for each attendant, and this includes, besides the lecture, the right to attend the class, to have an essay corrected, in most cases to sit for an examination, and, if successful, to receive a

[1] Cf. p. 91.

certificate. In the case of the Oxford courses it further includes the use of a small library.

We venture on the assertion that University Extension, as it exists, is one of the cheapest educational institutions in the country. At how small a relative cost it could be made one of the most efficient is indicated by the estimate given in Chapter III. for the maintenance of a University Extension College.

The greater portion of the annual expenditure of the University Extension authorities is for the payment of lecturers and examiners. So far as we know, the payment of all lecturers, except those employed in the County Council work, is by fees, and not by stipend. A very important change, tending to make the position of the lecturer more attractive to able men, has been made in the year 1890-91. It has long been felt that the permanent prosperity and usefulness of University Extension largely depends on the retention of the services of experienced and successful lecturers. Over and over again the leading lecturers have been offered, and many have been fain to accept, employment at much higher stipends in other work. The system cannot afford these repeated losses of the men who have served their apprenticeship and are coming to maturity. Such losses break the tradition of the work; they cause grievous waste of authoritative experience. And yet, unless University Extension lecturing can be made a possible profession for married men, they are inevitable. It has been clearly seen for some time that, until this defect is remedied, the best efforts to advance the system in other respects will be thrown away, and an attempt was therefore

Remuneration of the Lecturers.

made some two or three years ago to raise a fund, by private subscription, for the purpose of providing additional payments for the senior lecturers. That plan has, however, practically failed, and the only course that remained was to raise the fees charged to the local organisers for the services of the most experienced lecturers. This was sanctioned by the Oxford Delegates, tentatively in 1890, on a larger scale in 1891, and the result has abundantly justified the experiment. The Oxford Lecturers are now divided into three classes: Staff-Lecturers, Lecturers, and Junior Lecturers, and the fees are graduated in a corresponding manner. An ordinary Lecturer receives the same emoluments as before the change, but those of a Staff-Lecturer are increased, and those of a Junior Lecturer diminished.

Oxford Lecturers, Reserve Fund.

It is clear, however, that a lecturer's position is still a precarious one. A well-known and experienced lecturer is, of course, as sure of getting engagements as a successful barrister is of getting briefs. But the lecturer's income leaves no very large margin, and an illness, temporarily disabling him from giving lectures, would be a serious matter to him. If incapacitated during part or the whole of the winter, he would lose a large portion of the income on which he depends for the entire year. In view of this difficulty some friends of the Oxford branch of the movement—and among them one of its most generous supporters, Lord Ripon—are subscribing to a Lecturers' Reserve Fund, which will be available for the temporary aid of lecturers in case of illness. This fund already amounts to £400.

We have now completed our sketch of University Extension as it is. We claim that it contains all the elements required in a great teaching system, the personal touch with the teacher, the reading of selected books, the writing of essays and their criticism, discussion in the class and in the Students' Association, the test of the examination. It includes even the nucleus of a system of residence in the midst of academic surroundings. It does all this at a very small cost. The weak points in the scheme are the lack of sequence in the subjects of the courses; the fact that, comparatively speaking, so few young men attend the lectures; and, above all, the small degree to which the system has been made available for the working classes, despite the fact that, under occasionally fortunate circumstances, they have shown that they might be its most enthusiastic supporters. All three weak points are ultimately due to the difficulties of men and of money. These will be considered presently. With money the courses might succeed one another in regular educational sequence. If the courses were in sequence, and if the lecturers could be retained through their prime, when they had gathered experience and power of speech, more young men might be attracted. With such lecturers, and with money to cheapen the courses, the working classes would be reached.

The Merits and Demerits of University Extension as it is.

CHAPTER III.

UNIVERSITY EXTENSION: THE FUTURE.

IN the foregoing pages we have sketched the system of University Extension as it now exists, and have traced its growth from small beginnings to its present magnitude. It has been successful beyond the expectation of its most ardent supporters. Is it, however, destined to take its place among the permanent institutions of the country? Or is it merely a mushroom growth, which will die down and disappear? Has its rapid development been due to the fact that it both meets and stimulates a real demand in the country for higher adult education, or merely to novelty, which will fade away, and to the ardour of a few men who will forsake it? Such are the questions which are being asked by many competent observers, some of whom, while friendly to the movement, are still a little distrustful of its future.

There seems beyond doubt to be a steady and growing demand for the kind of instruction given by the University Extension system. At a large number of centres systematic courses of lectures have been arranged by the various University authorities during the last six winters without a break, while in a not inconsiderable proportion of towns University Extension work has gone on without flagging for over ten years. The number of candidates entering for the examinations steadily grows; the standard of their attainments seems as steadily to rise; and there is a marked increase in the number of students at the Summer Meetings. These facts convince all who are intimate with the movement that the interest and industry of the existing students show no sign of abatement, and that each year is adding largely to the numbers of those who are anxious to profit by the educational advantages of the system.

Its gradual establishment, however, on more permanent foundations and on a scale of wider usefulness can only be secured by the hearty co-operation of the Universities, of the local organisers, and, in our judgment, of the State. So far as concerns the students, the future of University Extension seems assured; it is largely on the other three factors that the prospect of its further development depends.

The Universities are able to supply the system with its best teachers, to guide it by their experience in organisation, to encourage its students by sympathy, and to test their attainments by wise and searching examination. The local organisers, acting in concert with the Universities, are enabled, by their intimate knowledge of their several neighbourhoods, to adapt the system to the various requirements of the different localities. The State, by giving recognition to the system, can lend it dignity, and, by a judicious measure of financial aid, can promote its efficiency without interfering with the liberty or relaxing the energies of its individual supporters.

The Three Chief Factors in the Future Development of University Extension.

I. **The Universities.**—The Bishop of London, speaking from his long experience in this side of University work, told the Oxford Conference in

I. The Universities can supply—

(a) Central Organisation. 1887 that "what is now particularly wanted is really good organisation."[1] Organisation alone could not have created the University Extension movement, but without organisation its system could not be maintained. The success of any scheme, which attempts the solution of one of the many problems of national education, depends in the first instance on the selection of a wise procedure; on the incessant improvement of methods; on numerous, and by no means invariably successful, experiments; on the careful tabulation of results; on the interchange and diffusion of varied experience. Especially in the early years of the system, many of its most pressing difficulties will be those of organisation. Organisers are needed both in the local centres and in the central offices, but it is obvious that it is on the latter that chiefly devolves the duty of giving advice to those who are inexperienced in the practical working of the system. Of the duties of the central organisers, however, nothing further need be said here except that their work is not without difficulty; that the success of the system largely depends on its manifold details being attended to with punctuality, accuracy, and method; that it is desirable for the organisers to be acquainted with the needs and circumstances of different parts of the country, and with the kind of men who will suit these different conditions; that there is need for thought in adjusting the machinery of the system to meet new wants; and that an undertaking which depends on the punctual working of most of the railway lines in England, and on the health, during the least clement season

[1] "Report of Oxford Conference on University Extension," 1887, p. 27.

of the year, of nearly a hundred lecturers, cannot fail to be prolific of emergencies.

Nor need much be said of the services rendered to the movement by the Universities in regard to examinations. At the end of each course the University audits, so to speak, the lecturer's accounts. An independent examiner weighs the attainments of those students who submit themselves to the test, and his report, endorsing, in all but an insignificant proportion of cases, the lecturer's commendations, or confirming his censures, gives an official seal to the educational thoroughness of the system. (*b*) Examinations.

No less noteworthy, however, is the stimulus which the Universities are in a position to give to the studies of those attending Extension courses. The high place held by the Universities in the public estimation; the dignity of their venerable associations; the warm and personal attachment which is now felt for them by increasing numbers of students previously outside the sphere of their influence; the generous and valued hospitality which they offer on the occasion of the Summer Meetings, all contribute to strengthen year by year the profound influence which is being exercised by the Universities on the spirit and ideals of the new movement for the diffusion of higher education. (*c*) Stimulus.

But by far the most important contribution which the Universities are making to the new system is the supply of lecturers. If there is one thing which, above all others, University Extension needs, it is a steady succession of the right kind of teachers, and it is in the Universities, if anywhere, that such teachers will be found. The (*d*) Lecturers.

Universities are engaged in the discharge of a traditionally double function—research and the teaching of teachers. Among the latter will always be found men who are fitted by gifts, knowledge, and inclination to find their widest opportunity of useful service as University Extension lecturers.

Nevertheless, it is clear that University Extension teaching is a special kind of work, and it follows that the man who is fully to succeed in it will need a combination of qualities. It is in reality a new profession, and cannot be casually recruited from among those who feel themselves unlikely to succeed in any of the more recognised callings. University Extension is, in fact, in competition with the other professions for the services of the best men whom the Universities turn out. It is an occupation which must always tax the strength and the resourcefulness of the men who engage in it. And, while this will be the case even when the work has settled down into a more humdrum stage, it is yet more true of the present time, when it has still to be pushed forward as an experimental scheme, and while large sections of the public have to be convinced of its usefulness. Moreover, the lecturers are called upon to represent their University in a very conspicuous manner. As the Vice-Chancellor of the University said at the Extension Conference held in Oxford in 1887, "The lecturers whom we send through the country are a kind of missionary; wherever they go, they carry on their foreheads the name of the University they represent. To a great many of those persons with whom they come in contact, it is the only opportunity afforded of learning what Oxford means and what is meant by the powers of an Oxford education."[1] It is of the highest importance, therefore, that the profession of University Extension teaching should command and attach to itself the services of men who are not unworthy to represent the University.

A man who is choosing his work in life naturally considers two things: his own special qualifications, and the career which is offered by the calling for which those qualifications seem to fit him. Our attention is now claimed by the qualifications which are desirable for the career of a University Extension lecturer.

In the first place, any lecturer who is to take an active part in the work must be strong enough to bear considerable fatigue. His occupation entails long and frequent journeys. In the future, the amount of travelling may, in the case of some of the lecturers, be reduced to a minimum; groups of neighbouring towns, separated from one another by short distances only, may combine together to retain for brief periods the whole time of a small staff of lecturers. Those whom the Master of Balliol once compared to "local preachers" may thus receive appointments to special "circuits" for a short term of years. But it will always be incumbent on some of the lecturers, and it is now incumbent on all of them, to make long journeys from one centre to another. It is this need of considerable physical strength which makes it doubtful whether many women—admirably adapted as some of them have proved to be for the work—will ever be able to undertake much of it or to make it their chief occupation. Moreover, the task of repeatedly

Summary of the Qualifications needed by a Lecturer.

[1] Report of a Conference in Oxford on the Extension of University Teaching. Oxford, 1887, p. 30.

lecturing to large audiences involves strain and excitement. The very intensity of the interest which the good lecturer takes in his work carries with it the danger of over-stimulation and consequent reaction.

Next, on the side of knowledge, the lecturer must possess some University distinction as evidence that he is competent to teach the subject or group of subjects on which he proposes to lecture. It is, however, the man of sound knowledge and many interests, rather than the learned specialist, who is needed for the work of University Extension. Mere knowledge of his subject is not enough. He will often have to lecture to people who need convincing that it is a subject of interest and importance to them. In order, then, to realise the best way of teaching it, he must be able to put himself in their place; he must be capable of taking an outside view of his subject. He must also be able to make his hearers feel the place which it occupies in the wide field of knowledge; he must know how to appeal to the varied information possessed by an audience consisting largely of adults, in such a way that each may find in his previous knowledge a foundation for his new study. The lecturer does not deal with children, but with grown men and women. He must therefore make their practical experience of life tell on the subject which he commends to their attention.[1] Further, he must seek to communicate to his students a correct impres-

---

[1] This is particularly necessary in the case of the lecturers engaged under the County Council schemes, who are dealing in many centres with audiences quite unprepared by any previous book-learning, and therefore only approachable through the medium of their own practical experience

sion of the different importance of the different parts of his subject; he must have instinctive tact in selecting salient points.

But he often has to address large audiences, and not merely to teach in small class-rooms, where a conversational method of instruction is suitable. He must, therefore, have some of the powers which go to make a good platform-speaker. He cannot afford to weary his hearers, for they are not compelled to come to listen to him again. It is his difficult task to combine the lucidity and force of good platform-speaking with the accuracy and precision of language which characterise the scholar.

His success as a teacher will depend on his convincing his audience that he is in intellectual sympathy with them. It will not do for him intellectually to despise them. He is facing an audience which comprises persons whose experience has lain in channels of which he himself knows little or nothing. In a sense, he is a specialist in one subject, addressing persons who are themselves specialists in fifty others. The relation, then, between the lecturer and his audience is rightly one of mutual respect. There will be many among his hearers who have been compelled by other claims, of business life or of household duty, to forego the opportunities for study which he himself has enjoyed. But this does not mean that they have experienced in their lives none of the mental discipline, the concentrated application, the need of judgment and criticism, which have been the forces education has brought to bear on his own life. Above all things, the lecturer must have moral earnestness, and must care deeply for the subjects which he teaches. He must, therefore, have a high ideal of the responsibilities and possibilities of his occupation.

He will have to come in contact with many different classes of people; he will often have to lecture to ladies in the afternoon and to working-men at night. This will call for a good deal of skill in handling his subject, so as to present it in a form suitable for both kinds of audience. It will not do for his lectures to be stereotyped.

Again, in many places his advice will be sought on matters of organisation. The most successful lecturers have been those who, like Mr. Moulton, of Cambridge, have given great attention to the practical means of arranging associations of students, federations of centres, and other matters which, though primarily concerned with the business side of the work, are still of importance to the teacher, because they consolidate the system in which he is employed, or improve the material with which he has to deal. A lecturer with a turn for organisation will thus find constant opportunities for usefully employing it. University Extension, in a word, needs men who belong exclusively neither to the academic nor to the business worlds, but who can sympathise with the aims and interests of both.

Such is the kind of lecturer that is wanted for the purposes of University Extension. It will be said at once that it is out of the question to hope for such paragons; that they do not exist; and that, if they did, the life of University Extension has nothing in it to tempt them. Our answer to this criticism must be that we are only describing an unattained ideal. We have stated the qualities which it is desirable that the ideal lecturer should possess. We are far from saying that University Extension is a forlorn hope unless every lecturer possesses all of them.

A good deal can be done by having something to aim at. When a man takes up University Extension lecturing, he is bound to be rather in the dark as to what is expected of him, and rather at a loss to know how best to prepare himself for a work of which he can only guess the difficulties. It is, therefore, important to consider how such a man can be helped. Can he serve an apprenticeship which will teach him his business? Can he be given anything worthy of the name of training? Can a supply of good lecturers be artificially created? Or is it wholly a question of temperament and natural gifts, which no training can give?

The truth probably is that without certain natural qualifications a man can never become a good lecturer; and some few men may, perhaps, be gifted enough to dispense with any formal training. Their earlier experience may have been of a kind to prepare them for this special work. But, in the case of the majority, it seems reasonable to suppose that a method of training could be devised which would develop natural gifts and make good material into better. *The Training of Lecturers.*

Such training, however, is beset with many difficulties. No University Extension centre likes to be practised on. When a committee pay for a lecturer, they naturally want a man who knows how to do his work. Therefore, when a lecturer accepts an engagement, he must go out ready to succeed. But this is like telling him that, when he is thrown into the water, he must be able to swim. Something may be done, of course, by charging different fees for different lecturers according to their experience. But it so happens that the towns which find it most difficult to raise funds for Extension Lectures are generally those for which an experienced lecturer is most needed. Again, when the local promoters are new to the work, they want a man who knows how to help them by the practical suggestions which a young lecturer is less able to make. And the probability is that, in the case of a centre which has only been established with difficulty, the lecturer will have to deal with an audience needing a kind of lecture which it is extremely hard to give. It is an old saying that a man must know a great deal of his subject before he can teach the elements of it. A young lecturer, fresh from his studies, is almost always more difficult to follow than one who has more knowledge and experience. He has not yet learnt what to leave out. The danger of charging lower fees for young lecturers is that the very centres which need an experienced man may content themselves with comparative inexperience because it is cheaper. On the other hand, it is obviously reasonable that the fee paid for a lecturer should bear some sort of relation to his experience and merit. The local committee which engages and pays for him hopes to recoup itself by the sale of tickets of admission to the lectures. It is clear, therefore, that an attractive lecturer at a high fee may be in the end as cheap as a less attractive lecturer at a lower one. The practical upshot of these considerations is that different fees are rightly charged for lecturers of different experience, but that it would be a mistake to offer, even at the lowest fee of all, a class of lecturers who had still to learn the rudiments of their business. Every one who goes out to lecture must somehow or other have learnt his trade.

But how can he learn it without accepting an ordinary paid engagement? It may be pointed out that many a man accepts a post as a schoolmaster who has never done any teaching. Why should not then a lecturer accept an engagement before he has done any lecturing? The answer to this lies in the difference between the positions of a lecturer and a schoolmaster. The latter is usually engaged for a considerable period—a term or a year. His employer thinks it worth his while to put up with a possible period of inefficiency, trusting that afterwards the services of the newcomer will compensate for previous waste; but the untrained lecturer is only invited to give, say, six lectures, or, at most, twelve. However quickly he learns his work, he will be almost at the end of his course before he has understood the best way to deliver it. Then, the young schoolmaster is only one of a staff of teachers; he finds himself one of a combination; his own work is only part of a great organised effort of teaching; the experience of his senior colleagues makes up for his own want of experience; he can get advice from them; the efficiency of the school is not simply dependent on him. The young lecturer, on the other hand, has to stand alone; whatever he does is bound to be noticed, and the fortunes of the course rest, so far as teaching goes, on his unaided exertions. Yet again, the young schoolmaster is dealing with pupils whose attendance is compulsory; they have not themselves paid to be taught by him; they sometimes even derive satisfaction from his inexperience. The young lecturer, on the contrary, addresses voluntary hearers ; if they are wearied by him, the remedy is in their own hands : they need not come again.[1]

In training himself for the special work of University Extension a man has another great difficulty to overcome. He has to teach himself to speak well in public. This may be scouted as impossible. But it should be observed that we are not requiring from him any remarkable gift of eloquence. If he happens to have such a gift, so much the better. All that is absolutely wanted from a lecturer is that he should be able to put his thoughts into clear and forcible words, to arrange his points in logical order, and to speak them from a platform in a way to which it is pleasant to listen. Higher gifts of speech than this may be born in a man, but not made by him. The art, however, of straightforward and effective platform-speaking is one that probably almost any man, who has the necessary physical qualifications and the necessary perseverance, can attain for himself. It is obvious, however, that it will be a help to him if he has been trained to face an audience, and to address it. In this matter, it would appear that the ordinary Englishman enjoys fewer advantages than the ordinary American. The American schoolboy is trained for public speaking. In his interesting *Notes on American Schools and Training Colleges*,[2] Dr. Fitch quotes the following passage from the programme of one

[1] It is worth noting that, even in the case of schoolmasters, the need of training is being felt. At more than one public school experiments are being made in this direction.

[2] Report of the Committee of Council on Education. London, 1889. Appendix to Mr. Fitch's Report, p. 500.

of the Normal Schools in Massachusetts:—"No efforts are spared to train the pupils in self-reliance. It is to this end that special importance is attached to platform exercises. These occupy a half-hour or so every day, and during this period pupils volunteer, each for five minutes or more, to read, or recite, or talk to the school upon any subject which they may have chosen. At such a time they have constantly to meet the criticism and questions of teachers and fellow-pupils; and thus the exercise has been found to be valuable, not only in training the pupils to use the English language with facility and force, and to speak with distinctness and accuracy, but in bringing them face to face with the sort of difficulties that they may be expected to meet in their profession."

In the University itself it is easy for a man to train himself by speaking to large gatherings. There are indeed no audiences in England to which it is better practice to speak than those which assemble for the weekly debates in the University Union Societies. The value of the experience gained in addressing them lies in the fact that they do not hesitate to express their feelings. But of late years, in Oxford at all events, it has become less the rule for a man with a turn for public speaking to go to the Union. A great number of small debating societies have sprung up in the different colleges. Men feel it perhaps more patriotic to support these college societies. They find themselves among friends. It is also less of an effort to address a small society than the Union audience. Less trouble need be given to preparation. The speaker does not court public failure. But, for these very reasons, a man loses a great deal who confines himself to the smaller societies and does not venture to address the larger one. He often falls into a desultory, conversational style of speaking. He contents himself with a slipshod manner of speech, because he has never accustomed himself to conditions which, for success, require him to take a great deal of trouble, not only with what he says, but with how he says it.

Such are the chief difficulties in the way of training lecturers for University Extension. At Oxford there is yet another difficulty, which is not unimportant. This is the absence from the University curriculum for men (not for women) of any systematic training in English literature. Into this question, which has its controversial aspects, we do not propose to enter. We are not here concerned with the question of a School of Literature. We will only remark that the present arrangements of the University make it far more difficult to find a young man who is competent to lecture on literary subjects than on history, philosophy, political economy, or any branch of natural science.

The Oxford Method of Selecting Lecturers.

In spite of these obstacles, something has been done in Oxford to train lecturers for University Extension. When a young man thinks of seeking appointment as a lecturer he sends an application to the Delegates. He must have passed the examinations required for a degree. In order that the Delegates may satisfy themselves as to his competence to teach the subject which he offers, he gives a reference to his college tutor. The applicant also has to show that he has already lectured in public with success. If his application is entertained, he comes to the office, and is told all about the system. He reads the official papers. Generally he has an interview with a senior lecturer. He tries to put himself in touch with the work and to realise its conditions. Next he has to write a syllabus of a course of lectures. This is submitted to the criticism of an experienced lecturer. The applicant is then required to deliver in Oxford, to a private audience, a part or the whole of the course of lectures of which he has already compiled the syllabus. He is not paid for giving the lectures. They are sometimes given to a school, but usually to the Oxford Diocesan Training College for Elementary Teachers. He has there as his audience a number of students who are themselves being trained to teach. At the lectures someone representing the Delegates is present. After the lecture he frankly criticises the applicant, the criticisms of the staff of the Training College generally confirming his verdict. When the course is over, the candidate's application is again considered. If the trial course has gone badly, the candidate commonly himself withdraws his application, or asks that decision may be postponed until he has had further practice. If the course has been successful, and the candidate is approved, he revises his syllabus in the light of the experience which he has already gained. The applicant is then very strongly advised to visit certain typical centres and to see the senior lecturers at their work. His name is subsequently added to the list of lecturers, and his revised syllabus is printed for circulation among the local organisers.

Of course, this little experiment in the way of

training is very incomplete; but it serves as a rough-and-ready means of eliminating the unfit. It is true that the process greatly improves those who undergo it; but its chief advantage is that it picks out the men who are justified in seeking employment in University Extension.

<small>Financial Aspect of the Lecturer's Position.</small>

We have now described the teachers on whose services the future of University Extension depends. It is to be believed that there will always be forthcoming a number of suitable persons who care enough for national education to embark on the work. But the nature of the occupation is too arduous, its claims on time are too exacting, for it to be possible to depend on purely voluntary assistance. If the first requirement of University Extension is men, its second and consequent need is money to support their work. The engagement of lecturers at a regular stipend would conduce to the permanence and well-being of the system. At present a lecturer, unless his services have for some time been largely in request, can hardly venture to forecast the probable amount of his next year's income. It may be larger than before, or it may suffer a serious, though temporary, diminution. The amount depends wholly on the lecturer's receiving from the local organisers invitations to lecture. He may be morally sure that these invitations will come to him, but it is clear that the precariousness of the income derived from the work injuriously affects its status as a regular calling. The offer of the County Councils of stipendiary positions tenable for the whole of one winter, and, as it is reasonably expected, renewable in the case of successful teachers from year to year, has at once drawn into University Extension work a number of senior and experienced lecturers, who had previously felt themselves unable to resign appointments entitling them to a fixed salary.

In this connection we must allude to the financial relations which subsist between the Universities and their University Extension systems. It has been pointed out on an earlier page [1] that the Universities already contribute towards the expenses of the work. They provide the general secretaries, their clerks, and their offices. We have not before us the Cambridge accounts, but from the balance-sheets presented by the Delegates to the University of Oxford since 1886 it appears that the University does not contribute to the payment of the lecturers or to the local expenses of the work.

Financial Relations Between Universities and University Extension.

Some critics in the newspapers have held that the Universities should do more. It has, however, been pointed out that, as institutions, the Universities are poor when the heavy claims on them are considered. In 1887 the Secretary of the Cambridge Syndicate pointed out that "the University of Cambridge is poor in money."[2] In the same year the Vice-Chancellor of the University made a similar statement with regard to Oxford. "The University," he remarked, "is not a rich body in comparison to the demands made upon it."[3] The published accounts of the Universities entirely confirm these statements. The Universities have large incomes, but there are large established calls on those incomes, and it would be obviously un-

[1] P. 93.
[2] Report of Cambridge Extension Conference, 1887, pp. 71, 77.
[3] Report of Oxford Extension Conference, 1887, p. 28.

reasonable to expect them to bear any large part of the expense of an entirely new system of higher education, the beginnings of which are already organised in almost every large town in the country.

As, however, was pointed out on the same occasions, in matters of finance as well as in government, the Colleges are largely separate from the University. It is not impossible that some of the Colleges might be able to render financial aid to University Extension work.

In discussing this matter we would again remind the reader that we speak only in our individual capacity as members of the University. We feel, however, that it is better for us frankly to state our own opinion. In our judgment, University Extension work has claims on a larger measure of financial aid from either University funds or collegiate revenues. The University and the Colleges both gain by the movement. The Colleges have already found in it a means of employment for many of their younger graduates. The University, as a whole, derives from it a less obvious, but a far more important, advantage. The University and the Colleges are national institutions. On more than one occasion they have been subjected to the investigation of a Parliamentary Commission. In view of any possible legislation in the future, it can be of no small service to them to have drawn to themselves the attachment of classes of great political importance in the country. We can testify from our personal experience to the fact that in several districts a spirit of distrust and even of hostility is giving way to a new sentiment of affectionate regard.

II. The Local Organisers.—Local organisation obviously plays an important part in the University Extension system, and to the perseverance and indefatigable activity of many of the local committees much of the present importance of the movement is due. The work of local, as of central organisation, however, needs both men and money. With the growth of the system, the burden of local management becomes heavier year by year; and, though these labours are cheerfully borne, it is clear that they can only be supported through any long period of years by energetic, clear-headed, and business-like persons, supplied with paid clerical assistance for the discharge of the more mechanical duties of secretaryship, and constantly encouraged by the interest and co-operation of local colleagues.

The local organisers want money, because their financial position is at present in many places, if not precarious, at any rate unsatisfactory. We have said that each lecture costs the students a shilling a head. This is true, but only on an average. There are many places where the students are so few that the cost which falls on each of them is more than twice that amount. And not only many small towns, but wide districts, where the population consists chiefly of the working classes, are debarred from University Extension because of its expense. Even a shilling a lecture seems prohibitive to many working-men and to those dependent on them. Again, in almost every centre the promoters depend partly on subscriptions. In other words, the work, to a certain extent, depends on the contributions of those who do not themselves regularly attend the lectures—that is, on the educationally-minded and benevolent public.

Speaking broadly, then, the University Extension centres are not well off. There are enviable exceptions; but, taking the movement as a whole, there are not many local committees with a balance of £50 at their bankers.

This want of comfortable means is very bad for an educational work. It pinches it. It compels the local promoters to have an eye, not only to what is ideally best for their students, but also to what will be tempting to the public. It forces them sometimes to refuse the best thing, and to content themselves with some more attractive second-best.

This financial difficulty is really at the bottom of the failure of many centres to arrange the courses in a systematic sequence. They cannot afford to do so. They know that if they embarked on a three years' course of history or literature— such as the Extension is perfectly ready at any moment to provide, and thousands of the more zealous students are eager to undertake—they would frighten their public. Many people on whom they rely for the sale of a certain and necessary proportion of tickets would start back from the scheme as too arduous and prolonged. Such persons are a minority of the audience; but their subscriptions are necessary, and, therefore, their taste for variety has to be considered. And so, instead of definitely undertaking a three years' course of study, many local committees eschew sequence or disguise it. They either oscillate between history and literature, between science and arts, or they take first the history of a period, then its literature, then its economics, and so on.

There is something to be said even for the first of these plans, and much more for the second. Variety stimulates, and it is well to learn all about a period from every side; but, at best, either plan is a *pis aller*. And the pity of it is that it is adopted, not because the local committees always like such an arrangement best, but because their purses are not deep enough for anything else. It is want of money which chiefly causes want of educational sequence.

Of course, there are numerous exceptions. The Cambridge affiliated centres undertake excellent courses of systematic study extending over three or four years, and comprising six full courses of lectures on either Arts or Sciences, with two other full courses drawn from the complementary group.[1] And many of the Oxford and London centres have made a brave fight for sequence. The London Society has arranged a very good series of courses at Gresham College, which thus serves as a central meeting point for the London students.[2] Every year a larger number of Oxford centres succeed in attaining sequence;[3] but the struggle is a hard one.

And it must be admitted that, when a new centre begins, the most important thing of all is to get a good lecturer. For such centres a sequence of subjects is desirable, but a sequence of good lecturers is essential. However, when all is said, we are bound to admit that a broad defect of the University Extension system, as it stands to-day, is that the majority of centres cannot afford to

---

[1] Cambridge Reports, 1887-90.
[2] London Reports, 1888, 1889.
[3] Oxford Reports, 1887-90.

devote their whole energies to arranging courses in educational sequence.

If they had more money, they would do it at once. They want money, too, for other purposes. The labour of local organisation grows heavier year by year; it involves more clerical work; a good deal of it is necessary, but dull; it often has to be done under great pressure of time; it involves the collection of money. It would be difficult to praise too highly the devotion with which the Local Committees and their energetic secretaries have applied themselves to these tasks. They have cheerfully borne an ever-increasing burden of secretarial work. Nothing has proved their interest in the movement more clearly than the willingness with which they have sacrificed leisure to the needs of organisation. But, as the work grows, they begin to want help. Already in large centres they require clerical assistance. Many of the local secretaries, who are best fitted for the work by reason of their business experience or faculty for organisation, are very naturally otherwise fully occupied. Again and again it has happened that, after two or three years of excellent service, such a secretary has been obliged to resign. With paid clerical assistance, he might have continued to direct the local organisation for many years. Besides, a movement gains by having an office. An office keeps up the tradition of the work. One secretary resigns and another succeeds; the clerk maintains the routine. The office becomes a permanent centre, a nucleus for further extension.

What form such extension will take, it is still impossible for anyone to forecast with certainty or precision. Each year, however, enables us to see more clearly what useful developments are possible or likely in local organisation. It is probable that in the future there will be four main types of University Extension centres. In the poorer districts and suburbs of the great city, which already contains a University or University College, there can be little doubt that University Extension work will gradually be drawn into closer relations with the central institution. The second class of University Extension centre will be found in those towns which, though possessing no University College, contain a large number of the energetic students, for whose educational needs a most inadequate provision is at present made. Of this type of centre, in some respects the most important of all, we shall speak in detail presently. The third class of centre will be found in the still smaller towns, and will no doubt resemble the type which is at present most familiar to all engaged in University Extension. Unable to establish the system on a very permanent foundation, or to venture on any elaborate scheme of graded teaching, such a centre will nevertheless continue to derive benefits from the delivery in each year of one or more courses of lectures, supplemented by the work of the Students' Association, and, in the case of the more advanced students, by annual visits to one or other of the Summer Meetings. Villages will form the fourth type of centre, and there the work must necessarily be carried on more intermittently, with longer intervals of private study, directed by correspondence, guided, perhaps, by student-lecturers, and from time to time stimulated by a visit from the lecturer himself. It is possible that, just as the University College may aid University Extension

Possible Developments in Local Organisation.

work in its own vicinity, so the village centre will be brought into natural relation with a wealthier University Extension Committee working in some neighbouring town.

It is, however, in the second type of centre that during the past year the most encouraging progress has been made, and there are signs that in several towns inhabited by a population of forty thousand and upwards, University Extension work may within a comparatively short time be placed on a more permanent basis.

A "University Extension College."
We suggest to such centres the establishment of a University Extension College. By this term we mean a building containing two lecture-rooms, one designed for a large audience, the second for a smaller class; a students' reference library; a small laboratory; an office for the local secretary and his clerk; and a caretaker's house. Such an institution would, in the absence of a University College, render important service to the higher education of the town in which it was established. It would provide the town with a convenient and well-equipped centre for the kind of instruction which it is the aim of the University Extension movement to popularise throughout the country. It would be a common meeting-ground for students, and would tend to give continuity and thoroughness to their studies.[1]

It is proposed that the instruction in such a University Extension College should be given by the itinerant staff of lecturers, three or four of whom would visit the College in each week of the session.

[1] A plan for such a University Extension College was sketched by one of the present writers in an article on University Extension published in the *Paternoster Review* for December, 1890.

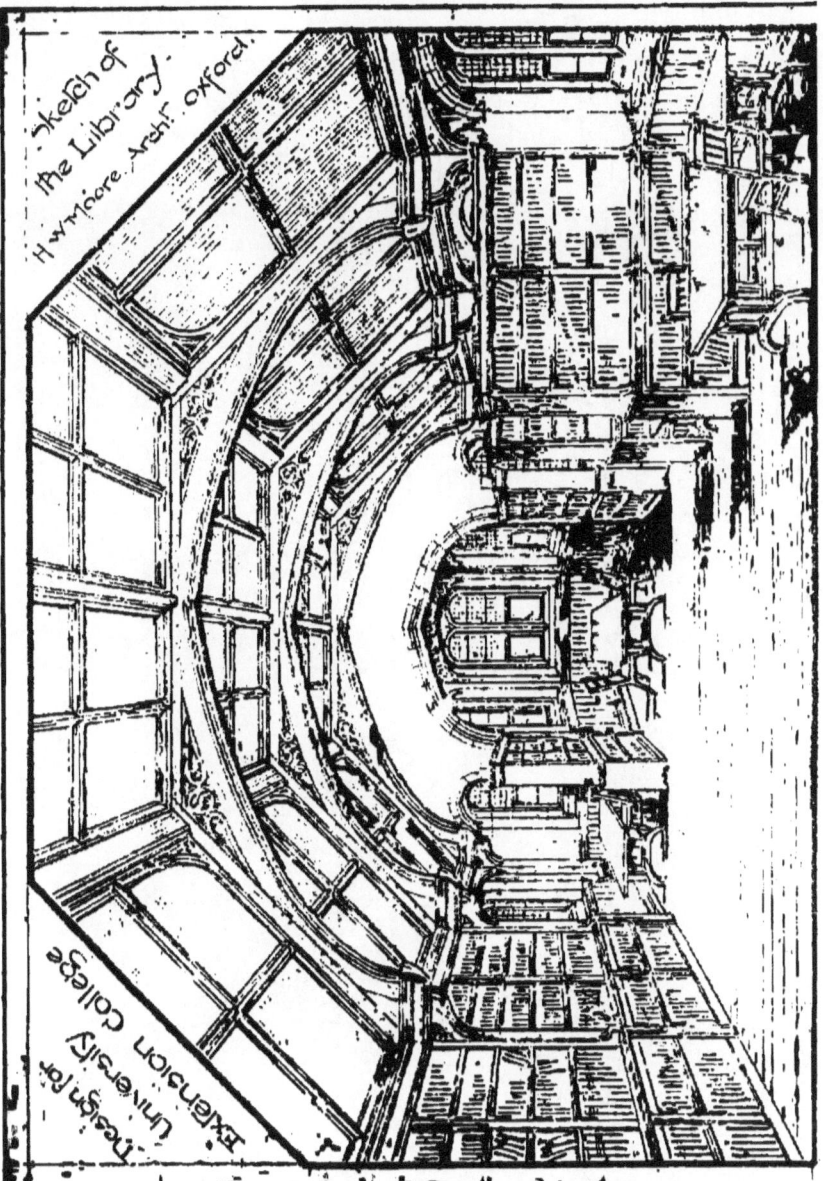

The College would be governed by the Local University Extension Committee, strengthened by representatives of the various public authorities of the town in proportion to the amount contributed by them to the funds of the institution. Established on such a permanent basis, the University Extension College might be affiliated, under existing statutes, to the Universities of Oxford and Cambridge, and it is conceivable that if any one of the Oxford and Cambridge Colleges happened to hold property in the town, a tie might naturally be formed between the mother and the daughter College.

This volume contains plans for such a University Extension College, designed by Mr. H. W. Moore, of Oxford. These plans are necessarily somewhat ideal, but they are intended to give a more vivid form to the scheme proposed above. It should be added that a local committee, by availing itself of existing rooms or premises, could often secure the substance of a University Extension College without going to the expense of a new building, and that in almost any case the details of the design would have to be modified in order to meet the special requirements of different sites.

The cost of such a College as that designed by Mr. Moore would be about £3,000. A further outlay of £500 would furnish the nucleus of the students' library, and equip the laboratory and lecture rooms with educational apparatus. A yearly expenditure of £600 would provide all the teaching, and pay the local secretary's clerk and a caretaker. This annual sum might be met by local subscriptions and fees amounting to £200, and by two allowances each of equal amount from the County or City Council (for scientific teaching) and from the Treasury

Grant for Local Colleges. Some of the expenditure might be saved if it were arranged that the scientific teaching, already established in most towns in connection with South Kensington, were brought into closer relation with the University Extension College.

DESIGN FOR UNIVERSITY EXTENSION COLLEGE.

DESCRIPTIVE NOTES.

The Design is illustrated by a sheet of plans, a view of the exterior, and a sketch of the interior of the Library; it must, however, be considered as somewhat tentative, for the planning of such a building would be greatly influenced by the facilities afforded by its intended site.

The accommodation includes :—

A large Lecture Room, to seat between 200 and 300.
A Room for Class Lectures, to seat about 60.
A Library.   A Working Laboratory.
Office for Secretarial purposes.
Caretaker's Residence ; and the usual Lavatories, etc.

The Lecture Rooms are arranged with a blank end-wall, for the use of the blackboard, diagrams, and lantern exhibits, and are lighted from the left side, which is preferable when circumstances will admit of it. In addition to its use for lecturing purposes, the Large Room would be available for conversaziones or other special gatherings.

The Library is shown to have the fittings arranged so as to form recesses for quiet study.

The Laboratory is approached by a separate flight of steps, to guard against laboratory smells permeating the building, and an enclosure is also provided for the requisite gas closets, etc.   North windows and roof lighting are highly desirable for this department, and it is advisable for it to be open to the roof for ventilating purposes.

The Secretary's Office is placed adjoining the entrance, to be handy for inquiries.

A side entrance allows of independent access to the Caretaker's residence.

Sketch Design for
University Extension College

Scale of feet

Heating Chamber,
Fuel and Stores
in Basement.

Ground Floor

Kitchen
Caretaker
Long Room
Yard
Lavy
Hall
Secretary's Office
Vestibule
Lecture Room
to seat
between 250-300

Upper Floor

Bedroom
Corridor
Bedroom
Landing
Laboratory
Class Room
to hold 60
Library

H. W. Moore FRIBA
Oxford

For Heating it is contemplated that a system of hot water or steam piping would be used, worked from an apparatus fitted up in the basement. Ventilation is another important detail which would require careful attention.

The design for the Exterior is intended for a red-brick building, with freestone dressings, and a tiled roof.

The approximate estimate of the cost of such a building amounts to £3,000.

     H. W. MOORE, Oxford,
      Fellow Royal Institute British Architects.

September, 1891.

There are many other purposes for which the Local Committee need money. It is right that they should always rely partly on local subscriptions, but they should not remain in bondage to them. They should be able, if necessary, to make arrangements long in advance without incurring rash liabilities. They should be free, so far as money goes, to seize chances of getting good lecturers. They should be enabled to supplement their popular courses with others of a tutorial character, more exclusively adapted for small classes of students. Each considerable town should have a variety of courses going on at the same time. Many brilliant teachers excel in inspiring small classes, but are ineffective when they deal with a large audience. It should be possible to make more frequent use of the services of such men in University Extension work.

It is clear that the local development of the work is hampered in every direction by want of means. We must therefore next consider the sources from which financial assistance for the local centres may be drawn. It may come from private munificence or from the State. In our judgment both sources should contribute a part. If it is urged that Uni-

The Sources of Financial Assistance for the Local Organisers.

versity Extension should be self-supporting, we must reply that throughout the whole of Higher Education in England part-endowment is the rule. No reason has yet been shown why University Extension should be treated as an exception.

Much has already been done for University Extension by the generosity of individuals. They have helped both the local committees and the central organisations. Private individuals have contributed to the Cambridge permanent fund.[1] Many others have given considerable sums to the Lecturers' Reserve Fund, established in connection with the Oxford branch.[2] Scholarships have been presented, and books have been given for the travelling libraries. The London Society has a considerable subscription list, to which some of the City Companies contribute. The Gilchrist trustees have voted considerable sums to the same Society, and have recently taken steps aimed at making their lectures preliminary to University Extension courses. In the future, donors may be forthcoming to endow lectureships or scholarships for their own counties or neighbourhood, just as professorial chairs have been established in the Universities and Colleges by private munificence.[3] While, however, it is to be hoped that the liberality of individuals will continue to help the movement, it must be admitted that up to the present the source of private generosity has not been sufficient adequately to supply its needs.

[1] Report of Cambridge University Extension Conference, 1887, p. 85.
[2] Oxford Report, 1889-90.
[3] Cf. the munificent donation mentioned on page 85.

III. **The State.**—We turn, therefore, to the consideration of the third possible factor in the future development of University Extension. It is in the power of the State to give dignity to the system without stereotyping it, and, by well-considered grants in aid, so to assist the local organisers as to stimulate them to even greater activity than they have already shown.

The time is now past when it was necessary, as a preliminary to any application for State aid, to discuss the whole question of the wisdom of State interference. So far, at any rate, as education is concerned, the principle has been granted many times over. As Professor Jowett has pointed out, "very nearly every civilised country in the world, France, Germany, Switzerland, and the United States of America, already provides education both primary and secondary, either free of cost, or at a very trifling cost, for all its citizens."[1] It is no leap in the dark which is proposed even as regards our own country.

Parliament annually votes several millions sterling in support of a system of elementary education, which is now in the main free to the public. It assigns in the same way large sums to Intermediate and Higher Education—to the Science and Art Department nearly half-a-million; to the Training Colleges for Elementary Teachers more than £100,000; to the London University nearly £15,000; to the Local Colleges of England £15,000 more; and there are grants besides to the Colleges and Universities of Wales, Scotland and Ireland. Large sums have recently been voted

[1] Report of Oxford University Extension Conference, 1887, p. 97.

to the County Councils for technical instruction. Any further employment of Government resources for purposes of education may be discussed, therefore, on grounds of justice and expediency rather than principle.

<small>The Justice of State aid to University Extension.</small>

Let us inquire, first, whether the people whom University Extension already serves and, were the necessary means forthcoming, could serve to a vastly greater extent than at present, have any claim on the ground of justice to the help of the State. If we examine the institutions which at present participate in the grants for higher educational purposes, we shall find that the London University is a purely examining body; that the Training Colleges are open only to candidates for one particular calling; and that the Science and Art Department teaches only certain subjects, and, to a large extent, teaches those, either directly or indirectly, for industrial purposes. The local colleges, on the other hand, receive help that they may better "discharge the duties which the title 'University College' implies;"[1] that is, that they may give above all things a higher general education. Part of the system by which they seek to discharge these duties consists of evening classes. Both as regards the social position of the students and the nature of instruction given, these evening classes—not to mention many of those held in the daytime—are almost precisely similar in character to those of the University Extension system. As we have seen, the local colleges arose from the same general movement which has given birth to the Extension. The Nottingham College, indeed, grew directly out of the Extension lectures which pre-

[1] See the Treasury Minute quoted on pp. 136-9.

ceded it, and is still largely served by the Cambridge Extension Lecturers. But the local college is a development of Extension teaching only possible in very large towns. Without the Treasury grant, it is more than doubtful whether places as large as Sheffield, Nottingham, and Bristol could have continued the costly luxury of an independent professoriate. Including the constituent colleges of the Victoria University and the two great Metropolitan Colleges, there are in all England and Wales only thirteen or fourteen such institutions, but there are nearly 350 towns of more than 10,000 inhabitants. It is at present impossible for the great majority of even earnest and self-denying students to attend lectures at a college. The great area covered by our chief cities often renders it difficult for those who live no further away than the suburbs, to make use of the city college. The teaching must be taken to the people where the people cannot come to the teaching. The local college is the form taken by the Extension system under peculiarly favourable circumstances. The whole body of taxpayers contribute to its maintenance, but only a very small percentage can make any use of it. The remainder of the Extension system works in the face of very great difficulties, but it reaches a larger body of the taxpayers than do the fixed colleges.

These colleges do a most valuable work, but the many small, and even moderately large towns scattered about the country get from them hardly any direct benefit in return for the contributions they make towards their support. Surely the Extension system, which can be made to furnish something like a University College by co-operation of smaller towns, is, in justice to those smaller towns, entitled to assistance from the State analogous to that accorded to the University Colleges.

<small>Objections to State aid for University Extension.</small> But it is objected the University Extension centres have no permanent organisation. They consist of committees and secretaries giving voluntary service, and are at any time liable to perish. They have no endowments, no salaried officers, no buildings, nothing in fact that guarantees continuance, and nobody to be made responsible for the right spending of the national funds. We admit the difficulty. But instability is not inherent in the University Extension system. If encouraged to do so, a large number of local committees would establish their work on a permanent basis. But such a step would entail a great effort, and we contend that it is unreasonable to ask small and often poor places to make such an effort, unless they have some security that the effort, once made, will not be left to die away during years of fruitless agitation. First let the State lay down the terms on which its help will be given, and many centres will soon comply with those terms. England was not covered with Science and Art teaching before the Department had stated the conditions on which it would recognise and aid it.

Some, on the other hand, object to State aid for University Extension because they fear the effects of Government interference. They are impressed with the dangers of departmental officialism, and point out that after a century of centralisation, France is now compelled to reverse her University policy. The one State University, managed from Paris, is about to give way to the revived independence of the Local Faculties. That, at any rate, is generally believed to be the meaning of the ministerial statements at the celebration held at Montpellier in 1890.

Others, again, dread the stereotyping of the present machinery, and argue that a system controlled by a "Department" is likely to lose its elasticity and adaptiveness, prime necessities of any educational machinery which is not ultimately to do more harm than good.

Lastly, we are told that the effect of grants from the State will be to remove the stimulus to local exertion and to stop the flow of private munificence.

These objections are all of the highest value as warnings, and must be borne carefully in mind by those who have the granting of the State's aid, and by those who will have the guidance of the system when that aid has been given. They have been constantly urged ever since the subject of State aid for University Extension was mooted, in 1889, at a conference of local secretaries and others present at the Oxford Summer Meeting. A scheme for capitation grants similar to those of the Science and Art Department was rightly rejected by the Conference because of criticisms on the above grounds, and a small committee was appointed to investigate the whole question. At a subsequent meeting of the conference, that committee presented the following preliminary report:— *The Origin of the Movement for State aid.*

"Parliament has recently granted a sum of fifteen thousand per annum to the local colleges of England. These colleges are situated in a few of the great centres of population. The result is that inhabitants of smaller places, while contributing to this sum, receive little advantage from it. The University Extension System is practically the local college of the smaller places. Upwards of thirty thousand students availed themselves of the advantages which it offered during the past year. This result has been attained at an average total cost of about ten shillings per student. The system is approved by the experience of seventeen years. It is capable of great development, and the time has come when it should be placed on a permanent footing.

"The State is spending upwards of three millions a year on elementary education. Five thousand a year granted to the Extension movement would greatly increase the benefits derived by the nation from that immense outlay. It is proposed that an application be made to Parliament for some such grant.

"The method employed in the distribution of the money among the centres might be that at present in force in the case of the local colleges. The grant would be entrusted to a central committee appointed by Government, and would be by them distributed amongst the local centres. The amount allotted to each would probably depend on such considerations as the following:—The nature of the population of the district, the amount of local subscriptions, the number of students, and the character and excellence of the work done."

The National Committee.

This report was adopted, and a larger committee composed of representatives both of the Oxford and the Cambridge movements was elected and styled the "National Committee for obtaining a Grant in aid of University Extension." The joint hon. secs. of the committee were Mr. H. Macan, of Exeter, and Miss Snowden, of Ilkley, Yorkshire, and under their energetic lead the subject was steadily kept before the centres, and brought to the attention of members of Parliament with a view to the ripening of public opinion.

The one-sided nature of the endowment given by the "spirit-money."

In July, 1890, came the unexpected windfall of the "spirit money." For reasons which have been referred to in the last chapter, the University

Extension authorities at once saw the advisability of undertaking instruction of a more technical character than that which they had previously given, with the result that the scientific subjects, which are now practically State-aided, threaten to oust History and Literature from their due share of attention. There is only one way in which the balance can be restored, and that is by giving similar assistance and encouragement to historical, literary and economic studies. The part which these studies play in the education of good citizens makes the demand for their encouragement by the State quite as legitimate as in the case of elementary and technical subjects. The simplest plan would be to extend the discretion given to the County Councils by enabling them to subsidise teaching in all, and not merely in technical, subjects. It is very doubtful, however, whether under the conditions just now prevailing the results of such a policy would be satisfactory. A large number of the County Councils have already framed new schemes with definite technical objects, and have adjusted their machinery for the realisation of those schemes. Several years must elapse before the country will be able to judge the results of the various experiments thus undertaken. The effect of thrusting new educational duties upon the County Councils at the present moment would be to produce confusion. Schemes, originally intended for technical teaching, would be warped by having new and incompatible plans grafted on to them. Organising secretaries, appointed because of their special fitness for certain duties, might be called upon to carry out duties for which they are not specially prepared. More-

J

over, it must be remembered that the sudden demand for teachers during the past summer has greatly strained the resources of the various bodies whose function it is to supply such teachers, and this, too, although the wants of different localities varied according to their different trades and industries. In such subjects as History and Literature, the demands from the various parts of the country would differ in character but little, and would be addressed, moreover, far more exclusively to the Universities than in the case of scientific and technical subjects. Were the powers of the County Councils suddenly widened in the direction indicated, there would be far more danger of the engagement of a number of inferior and inadequately-trained teachers, who might easily discredit the whole scheme, and make the retrieval of the false start a terribly up-hill task.

A small and temporary Treasury Grant suggested for the encouragement of studies not covered by the County Council grant.

We believe, therefore, that it would be best to leave the County Councils undisturbed while they grapple with the organisation of technical education, adopting in the meantime temporary measures in regard to what is commonly called "liberal" education. A comparatively small grant direct from the Treasury, to carefully selected University Extension Centres and Federations of Centres, would lead to a steady and increasing demand for teachers of the very special type required. The University Extension authorities would then be able to undertake the task of training such lecturers, at the same time that able men would feel tempted to throw in their lot with the movement.

It cannot be too strongly emphasised that the number of men who can present precise and scholarly thought in plain and lucid language is limited, and that to collect a considerable staff of such men is a matter requiring several years of care and watchfulness. If the above plan were adopted, the County Councils would find the machinery ready to hand, organised and tested, whenever it seemed good to Parliament to delegate greater powers over education to the local authorities. Experiments would have been tried, experience accumulated, and a tradition built up, the like of which, if they had existed in technical subjects, would have saved much wasted trouble and money in the present juncture of affairs.

In order that such an experiment might be tried with the best chance of success, it would be necessary that financial aid from the State should be accompanied by the minimum of State interference. The time of capitation grants, with minute and rigid control and inspection, is passing away, and the newer and more trustful policy has nowhere been better expressed than by Sir William Hart-Dyke, the Vice-President of the Committee of Council on Education. Speaking at Ruthin, on August 11th of the present year, on the occasion of the laying of the foundation-stone of the new Grammar School, he said that " the Welsh people had got a start of England in regard to educational matters. They could command all their local energies and all their talents for the formation of educational schemes supported by the State, yet interfered with as little as possible by the State or any central body. He was one of those who believed in as little centralisation as possible in regard to educational questions."

The Minimum of State Interference.

The principle of leaving as much as possible to

local initiative and discretion is that which governs the relations of the Universities to the University Extension Centres, and it is this principle which ought also to govern the relation of the State to the same Centres. At the same time, the audit and publication of accounts is good for every public institution, whether State-aided or not. The University Extension Centres have shown marked anxiety to have their educational work audited by the University Examiners, and there could be no possible objection to an official audit of their finances. If, in some few cases, it compelled a little more care and accuracy than at present in the business management of the Centres, the movement as a whole would be the gainer.

A Precedent for the Scheme. The model upon which the scheme might be framed is to be found in the Treasury Minute of 1889, stating the conditions on which the sum of £15,000 would be distributed among the University Colleges of Great Britain.

It will be useful, therefore, to reproduce that Minute in full:—

"My Lords have had under their consideration the report of the Committee appointed to advise the Government with reference to the distribution of the sum of £15,000 which Parliament is to be asked to grant for.'.University Colleges in Great Britain.'

"The Committee state in their report that the sum assigned by them to each college is made up of two items— (*a*) a fixed sum to each college, together with a grant to the college for each professor or head of a department, and (*b*) a percentage on the total amount of local subscriptions and students' fees.

"My Lords believe that this system of distribution takes just account of the main factors which should, under existing circumstances, determine the share to be received by each University College out of any sum granted by

Parliament, and is a reasonable application of the general principles laid down in the memorandum of the Lord President and the Chancellor of the Exchequer. They accordingly accept the allocation of the grant of £15,000 for the present year as proposed by the Committee, viz. :—

	£
Owens College, Manchester	1,800
University College, London	1,700
King's College, London	1,700
Liverpool University College	1,500
Mason College, Birmingham	1,400
Yorkshire College, Leeds	1,400
Nottingham University College	1,400
Bristol University College	1,200
Durham College of Science (Newcastle-on-Tyne)	1,200
Firth College, Sheffield	1,200
Dundee University College	500

"My Lords recognise that the present allocation of the money is more or less experimental, and that experience may show that greater or less weight ought to be attached to one or other of the various items, such as extent of endowment, amount of fees, amount of local subscriptions, &c., upon a comparison of which in the different colleges the Committee have based their recommendations. In any case the relative claims of the several colleges upon the total grant will vary from time to time, and the allocation of that grant ought therefore to be subject to periodical revision. My Lords indeed feel that it would not be desirable to alter the amount of the subsidies received by the different colleges with such frequency as to produce constant uncertainty in their financial outlook. But neither would it seem wise so to stereotype those subsidies as to remove the incentive which they ought to afford to the spirit of self-help on the part of the colleges and their supporters. My Lords are of opinion that adequate regard would be had to both these considerations if the distribution of the grant of £15,000, should Parliament see fit to continue it, were liable to be reviewed every five years.

"The above remarks as to periodical revision do not, of course, apply to the University College of Dundee, inasmuch as, in accordance with the recommendations of the Committee, my Lords regard the grant to that institution as confined, in any case, to the present year.

"My Lords approve of the suggestion of the Committee that 'a person representing the Government should visit each college from time to time, not with a view of examining the students, but to inspect the buildings and laboratories and to become personally acquainted with the extent of the different courses of study.' The exact method of carrying out this recommendation is, however, a matter for future discussion between the Education Department and the Treasury.

"In addition to such periodical inspection, which my Lords believe will be welcomed by the colleges, it would seem reasonable to require that each college, so long as it continues to receive State assistance, should furnish annually to the Education Department a statement showing the result of the last academic year's work, and that such statement should contain, in particular, the number of professors and students and the average number of lectures attended by each student, the state of the college finances, distinguishing under the head of receipts between subscriptions, interest on endowments, fees, and other sources of revenue, together with such other information as might supply a general view of the academic achievements and financial position of the college.

"The continued participation of any particular institution in the grant for 'University Colleges in Great Britain' must, of course, depend upon the evidence forthcoming, in either of the above ways, or otherwise, of its continuing adequately to discharge the duties which the title 'University College' implies. While my Lords are of opinion that a general review, and, if need be, redistribution of the grant should not be undertaken oftener than once in five years, they are anxious clearly to establish the principle that no college is to be regarded as having a vested right to share, even for a limited number of years, in the sums voted by Parliament. On the contrary, each college should be considered as liable to be excluded at any time from further participation in the grant if it should appear to the Treasury and the Education Department that, owing to inadequacy of educational equipment, to a great falling off in the number of its students, or to any other cause, it had ceased to be deserving of support from the National Exchequer. But, of course, any proposed change in the distribution of the grant will not take effect until it has been brought to the notice of Parliament in connection with the estimate.

"In conclusion, my Lords desire to express their sense of the services rendered by the Committee, to whom the thanks of Her Majesty's Government are due for their careful investigation of the claims of the several colleges, and for the valuable suggestions contained in their report."

We are not aware that any complaints have yet been made on the part of the Local Colleges receiving the grants of undue Government interference.

It was to discuss a scheme of this character that a meeting convened by Mr. A. H. D. Acland, M.P., the Master of Christ's College, Cambridge, the Master of University College, Oxford, the Provost of Queen's College, Oxford, Professor Henry Sidgwick, Professor Max Müller, Dr. Percival, the Principal of Bishop Hatfield's Hall, Durham, Mr. J. G. Talbot, M.P., the President of Magdalen College, Oxford, and the Secretaries of the Cambridge Syndicate for Local Lectures, was held at the Westminster Palace Hotel, on Friday, June 5th, 1891. Among those present were Mr. James Stuart, M.P., Mr. J. G. Talbot, M.P., Sir Henry Roscoe, M.P., Mr. C. T. D. Acland, M.P., Mr. A. H. D. Acland, M.P., Mr. Grotian, M.P., the Master of Christ's College, Cambridge, the Provost of Queen's College, Oxford, the Master of University College, Oxford, the Rector of Exeter College, Oxford, Professor Henry Sidgwick, Canon Browne, the Secretaries to the Cambridge Syndicate, and to the Oxford Delegacy for Local Lectures, Dr. Spence Watson, Dr. Ginsburg, Mr. F. D. Mocatta, Mr. Walter Palmer (Reading), Mr.

The Meeting in London on June 5th, 1891.

H. Macan (Exeter), Mr. W. C. Pendarves, Mr. George Tayler (Guildford), Mr. Arnold-Bemrose (Derby), Mr. E. C. Sinkler (Lewisham), Miss Montgomery (Exeter), Miss Moberly (Tunbridge Wells), Mr. J. A. Round (Colchester), and Mr. Boaler (Horsham), besides several of the Senior Oxford and Cambridge University Extension Lecturers.

On the motion of Professor Sidgwick, seconded by the Rector of Exeter College, it was carried, with only three dissentients, "That it is expedient that a Government Grant be given to properly organised local bodies for the conduct of University Extension Teaching."

A draft scheme, prepared by the writers of this book, was then adopted as the basis of discussion. Its chief clauses, as amended by the meeting, were as follows :—

I. It seems expedient that such grants should be made on conditions which—
  (1) Would not involve the Government in the examination of an embarrassing number of claims ;
  (2) Would encourage systematic sequence of study ;
  (3) Would require any local committee, which received the grant, to be representative ;
  (4) Would not relax local effort.

II. These conditions would be met by the following plan :—
  (1) Grants to be made only to those local committees, or district federations of local committees, which should undertake to arrange an adequate minimum of courses of lectures and classes, with final examinations arranged in a sequence ensuring continuity of teaching and—
    (*a*) Extending over a period of years ;
    (*b*) Approved by the University Extension Authorities superintending the courses ;

(c) Comprising courses drawn from both the Arts group and the Science group, the latter to include some practical work in Science.

(2) The local committees of management should be representative of their localities;

(3) The Government Grant should provide part of the cost of the teaching, the residue being provided by local grants, subscriptions, etc. The Government to have the right at any time to inspect, by a specially appointed inspector, the work being done, with a view to ascertaining how far in its judgment the grants are properly expended;

(4) Each centre receiving aid to present annually to the Government an officially-audited balance sheet, and a report on the courses by the University Extension Authorities superintending them.

III. The University Extension Authorities mentioned above in II., (1) and (4), would at present include the Universities of Oxford, Cambridge, and Durham, Victoria University, and the Universities' Joint Board of the London Society for the Extension of University Teaching.

The subject was again discussed at a meeting of local organisers held during the recent Oxford Summer Meeting, the Marquis of Ripon being in the chair.

It only remains to add that in clause II. (1) of the scheme just quoted, the phrase " or district federations of local committees " was inserted to meet the views of some, who hold that a portion of any grant which may be made, ought not to be expended in raising the standard and amount of the work done in certain selected centres, but in making experiments of " a missionary character " in the mining and agricultural villages. Such experiments made with Government funds, would have to contend with difficulties which would not affect the remainder of the scheme, but if undertaken they would probably be best carried out by the District Federations or Associations mentioned in Chapter II. The work now being organised by the South Eastern Association for the County Council of Kent, anticipates, in some respects, no doubt, the kind of experiment contemplated.

Summary.

Finally, let us summarise the case for State aid to the general, as well as to the technical, side of University Extension teaching. Elementary education has made higher education indispensable, for the power of reading, unless accompanied by further training, is often a questionable advantage for the individual, and may, in certain circumstances, become a danger to the State. Higher education obviates these dangers by introducing new benefits. It gives intellectual interest to life and conduces to sobriety of political judgment. The study of national history and national literature cannot fail to inspire patriotism. In short, by giving contact with the greatest thoughts of the world, such training imparts higher ideals of life, of citizenship, and of religion, and is therefore as necessary to the well-being of a democratic state as technical training is to that of an industrial and commercial state.

Libraries alone, cannot give this training, for they merely bewilder the uninitiated and present no standard of attainments to the student. Personal teaching of a high and inspiring order is needed to make books speak with effect.

Great sums from the National funds, central and local, have been and are being spent on elementary education and on public libraries. It behoves the State, therefore, to see that much of this expenditure is not wasted because of a little incompleteness in educational machinery. If private agencies are insufficient for the purpose of completing it, then it is the duty of the State either to strengthen, or to supplant, those agencies, and we believe that where possible, the former is the better policy and more consonant with English practice. The agencies already at work are the Universities, the Local Colleges in the great towns, and the University Extension system of peripatetic teachers both in the smaller places and in the outlying districts of large cities. The Treasury already subsidises some of the Universities and most of the Local Colleges; the County Councils are in many parts of the country helping the scientific work of the University Extension system. Whatever may be the method of subsidy ultimately adopted, we believe, for reasons which we have already stated in full, that a small grant should be given in the first instance from the Treasury. We suggest that this should be looked upon as a temporary and experimental measure, to continue while the County Councils are gaining experience from the organisation of technical education, and while the University Extension Authorities, central and local, are adapting themselves to the changed conditions. It could be given, too, in such a manner as to stimulate local effort rather than to relax it, and we propose that, while the periodical audit of accounts should be reserved to the Government, the task of examination and of suggestion in educational matters should be entrusted to the Universities. By degrees, the great Universities might come to hold in educational affairs the same kind of official, yet detached, position, with reference to the Government as the Bank of England does in financial matters. In default of Government action the Universities by their Local and "Joint Board" examinations have already given a consistency and system to our secondary education which it totally lacked a generation ago. But the erection of what will be a great People's University, extending over the whole land, is beyond the unaided means of corporations whose endowments are already largely absorbed in other indispensable tasks. The State and the local benefactor must bear most of the financial burden of the new departure, but the Universities can contribute teachers, experience, organisation, traditions, and historic prestige.

NEW ISSUE NOW PUBLISHING IN WEEKLY VOLUMES, in Paper Covers, 3d., or Cloth, 6d.,
OF
CASSELL'S NATIONAL LIBRARY.
Edited by Professor HENRY MORLEY.

CASSELL'S NATIONAL LIBRARY is a literary enterprise unique in the annals of English publishing, and may fairly be said to mark

AN EPOCH IN THE PRODUCTION OF CHEAP LITERATURE.

Well did the *Athenæum* write of the series that "no greater feat has been accomplished during the last quarter of a century," and appropriately did the same journal characterise it as

"A WONDERFUL BARGAIN."

On several occasions HER MAJESTY THE QUEEN has graciously expressed the pleasure with which she viewed the publication of the series; whilst Statesmen, Educationists, Clergymen, and leading men in all Professions, have greeted its appearance with unanimous approval.

And, better still, all classes have read it, from the humblest workmen in the kingdom to the greatest students and ablest thinkers.

Mr. John Bright wrote specially to thank the publishers for "the service thus rendered to the education of the people by giving them so much that is of

INESTIMABLE VALUE."

Mr. Gladstone has several times expressed his appreciation of the Library, which he regards as

"A STEP IN ADVANCE."

"What a boon would be the perusal of, say, 'Cassell's National Library' alone!" remarked the *Illustrated London News*. "We hear a good deal about

THE HUNDRED BEST BOOKS.

Here we have a hundred best books which may be bought for less than a couple of pounds at almost any bookseller's."

In referring to CASSELL'S NATIONAL LIBRARY, *Punch* remarked that "the old proverb was 'Every Englishman's house is his castle.' In future this will be

'EVERY ENGLISHMAN'S HOUSE HAS HIS CASSELL.'"

This new proverb may practically be regarded as an accomplished fact, since literally MILLIONS OF VOLUMES of this Library have already been circulated, and the Works are now well known, not in Great Britain only, but in nearly every civilised country in the world.

In arranging for the new serial issue, Messrs. Cassell &

but they have decided to make a **Selection of the most Popular Works**, amongst which will be some valuable books that will now appear in this series for the first time. The following is the order of Volumes appearing in the New Issue :—

The Haunted Man	DICKENS.
Utopia	Sir T. MORE.
Lays of Ancient Rome	MACAULAY.
Essays on Burns and Scott	CARLYLE.
Wanderings in South America	WATERTON.
Heroes and Hero-Worship	CARLYLE.
Voyages and Travels	MARCO POLO.
Hamlet	SHAKESPEARE.
The Complete Angler	WALTON.
Essays Civil and Moral	BACON.
The Lady of the Lake	SCOTT.
Friends in Council	Sir A. HELPS.
The Autobiography of	BENJAMIN FRANKLIN.
Grace Abounding	BUNYAN.
The Rivals, and The School for Scandal	SHERIDAN.
Warren Hastings	MACAULAY.
Areopagitica, etc.	MILTON.
The Angel in the House	COVENTRY PATMORE.
Life of Nelson	SOUTHEY.
The Battle of the Books, etc.	SWIFT.
Merchant of Venice	SHAKESPEARE.
Sublime and Beautiful	BURKE.
Sir Roger de Coverley	STEELE and ADDISON.
Macbeth	SHAKESPEARE.
A Defence of Poesie	SIDNEY.
Paradise Regained	MILTON.
Christmas Carol, and The Chimes	DICKENS.
Antony and Cleopatra	SHAKESPEARE.
Childe Harold	BYRON.
Murad the Unlucky, etc.	EDGEWORTH.
Measure for Measure	SHAKESPEARE.
Lives of the Poets (Waller, Milton, Cowley)	JOHNSON.
My Ten Years' Imprisonment	SILVIO PELLICO.
Much Ado about Nothing	SHAKESPEARE.
Plays	OLIVER GOLDSMITH.
Tales from the Decameron	BOCCACCIO.
Julius Cæsar	SHAKESPEARE.
Visions of England	PALGRAVE.
Rasselas	JOHNSON.
Midsummer Night's Dream	SHAKESPEARE.
Paradise Lost (Two Vols.)	MILTON.
All's Well that Ends Well	SHAKESPEARE.
Knickerbocker's History of New York (Two Vols.)	WASHINGTON IRVING.
Sintram and his Companions	FOUQUÉ.
Henry VIII.	SHAKESPEARE.
The Memorable Thoughts of Socrates	XENOPHON.
Daphnaida, and other Poems	SPENSER.
King John	SHAKESPEARE.
Undine, and The Two Captains	FOUQUÉ.
Bravo of Venice	LEWIS.

The sixpenny volumes of this new edition are issued in tasteful cloth bindings, on which no advertisements appear.

* *Intending subscribers are requested to order the Volumes by* Name (*not by Number*), *and to ask for the* "*New Issue.*"

Selections from Cassell & Company's Publications.

Illustrated, Fine-Art, and other Volumes.

Abbeys and Churches of England and Wales, The: Descriptive, Historical, Pictorial. Series II. 21s.
A Blot of Ink. Translated by Q and PAUL FRANCKE. 5s.
Adventure, The World of. Fully Illustrated. In Three Vols. 9s. each.
Africa and its Explorers, The Story of. By DR. ROBERT BROWN, F.L.S. Illustrated. Vols. I. and II., 7s. 6d. each.
Agrarian Tenures. By the Rt. Hon. G. SHAW-LEFEVRE, M.P. 10s. 6d.
Anthea. By CÉCILE CASSAVETTI (a Russian). A Story of the Greek War of Independence. *Cheap Edition.* 5s.
Arabian Nights Entertainments, Cassell's Pictorial. 10s. 6d.
Architectural Drawing. By R. PHENÉ SPIERS. Illustrated. 10s. 6d.
Art, The Magazine of. Yearly Vol. With 12 Photogravures, Etchings, &c., and about 400 Illustrations. 16s.
Artistic Anatomy. By Prof. M. DUVAL. *Cheap Edition.* 3s. 6d.
Astronomy, The Dawn of. A Study of the Astronomy and Temple Worship of the Ancient Egyptians. By J. NORMAN LOCKYER, F.R.S., F.R.A.S., &c. Illustrated. 21s.
Atlas, The Universal. A New and Complete General Atlas of the World, with 117 Pages of Maps, in Colours, and a Complete Index to about 125,000 Names. Cloth, 30s. net; or half-morocco, 35s. net.
Awkward Squads, The; and Other Ulster Stories. By SHAN F. BULLOCK. 5s.
Bashkirtseff, Marie, The Journal of. *Cheap Edition.* 7s. 6d.
Bashkirtseff, Marie, The Letters of. 7s. 6d.
Beetles, Butterflies, Moths, and Other Insects. By A. W. KAPPEL, F.E.S., and W. EGMONT KIRBY. With 12 Coloured Plates. 3s. 6d.
"Belle Sauvage" Library, The. Cloth, 2s. each.

Shirley.	Adventures of Mr. Ledbury.	Jack Hinton.
Coningsby.	Ivanhoe.	Poe's Works.
Mary Barton.	Oliver Twist.	Old Mortality.
The Antiquary.	Selections from Hood's Works.	The Hour and the Man.
Nicholas Nickleby (Two Vols.).	Longfellow's Prose Works.	Handy Andy.
Jane Eyre.	Sense and Sensibility.	Scarlet Letter.
Wuthering Heights.	Lytton's Plays.	Pickwick (Two Vols.).
Dombey and Son (Two Vols.).	Tales, Poems, and Sketches. Bret Harte.	Last of the Mohicans.
The Prairie.	Martin Chuzzlewit (Two Vols.).	Pride and Prejudice.
Night and Morning.	The Prince of the House of David.	Yellowplush Papers.
Kenilworth.	Sheridan's Plays.	Tales of the Borders.
Ingoldsby Legends.	Uncle Tom's Cabin.	Last Days of Palmyra.
Tower of London.	Deerslayer.	Washington Irving's Sketch-Book.
The Pioneers.	Rome and the Early Christians.	The Talisman.
Charles O'Malley.	The Trials of Margaret Lyndsay.	Rienzi.
Barnaby Rudge.	Harry Lorrequer.	Old Curiosity Shop.
Cakes and Ale.	Eugene Aram.	Heart of Midlothian.
The King's Own.		Last Days of Pompeii.
People I have Met.		American Humour.
The Pathfinder.		Sketches by Boz.
Evelina.		Macaulay's Lays and Essays.
Scott's Poems.		
Last of the Barons.		

Biographical Dictionary, Cassell's New. 7s. 6d.
Birds' Nests, Eggs, and Egg-Collecting. By R. KEARTON. Illustrated with 16 Coloured Plates. 5s.
British Ballads. With Several Hundred Original Illustrations. Half-morocco, *price on application.*
British Battles on Land and Sea. By JAMES GRANT. With about 600 Illustrations. Three Vols., 4to, £1 7s.; *Library Edition,* £1 10s.

5 G. 11.93

Selections from Cassell & Company's Publications.

British Battles, Recent. Illustrated. 4to, 9s.; *Library Edition*, 10s.
Butterflies and Moths, European. With 61 Coloured Plates. 35s.
Canaries and Cage-Birds, The Illustrated Book of. With 56 Facsimile Coloured Plates, 35s. Half-morocco, £2 5s.
Capture of the "Estrella," The. A Tale of the Slave Trade. By COMMANDER CLAUDE HARDING, R.N. 5s.
Cassell's Family Magazine. Yearly Vol. Illustrated. 9s.
Cathedrals, Abbeys, and Churches of England and Wales. Descriptive, Historical, Pictorial. *Popular Edition.* Two Vols. 25s.
Catriona. A Sequel to "Kidnapped." By ROBERT LOUIS STEVENSON. 6s.
Celebrities of the Century. *Cheap Edition.* 10s. 6d.
Chips by an Old Chum; or, Australia in the Fifties. 1s.
Chums. The Illustrated Paper for Boys. First Yearly Volume. 7s. 6d.
Cities of the World. Four Vols. Illustrated. 7s. 6d. each.
Civil Service, Guide to Employment in the. 3s. 6d.
Climate and Health Resorts. By Dr. BURNEY YEO. 7s. 6d.
Clinical Manuals for Practitioners and Students of Medicine. A List of Volumes forwarded post free on application to the Publishers.
Colonist's Medical Handbook, The. By E. A. BARTON, M.R.C.S. 2s. 6d.
Colour. By Prof. A. H. CHURCH. With Coloured Plates. 3s. 6d.
Columbus, The Career of. By CHARLES ELTON, Q.C. 10s. 6d.
Combe, George, The Select Works of. Issued by Authority of the Combe Trustees. Popular Edition, 1s. each, net.
  The Constitution of Man. | Science and Religion.
  Moral Philosophy. | Discussions on Education.
                American Notes.
Cookery, A Year's. By PHYLLIS BROWNE. 3s. 6d.
Cookery, Cassell's Shilling. 384 pages, limp cloth, 1s.
Cookery, Vegetarian. By A. G. PAYNE. 1s. 6d.
Cooking by Gas, The Art of. By MARIE J. SUGG. Illustrated. 3s. 6d.
Cottage Gardening, Poultry, Bees, Allotments, Food, House, Window and Town Gardens. Edited by W. ROBINSON, F.L.S., Author of "The English Flower Garden." Fully Illustrated. Half-yearly Volumes, I. and II. Cloth, 2s. 6d. each.
Countries of the World, The. By ROBERT BROWN, M.A., Ph.D., &c. Complete in Six Vols., with about 750 Illustrations. 4to, 7s. 6d. each.
Cyclopædia, Cassell's Concise. Brought down to the latest date. With about 600 Illustrations. *Cheap Edition.* 7s. 6d.
Cyclopædia, Cassell's Miniature. Containing 30,000 subjects. Cloth, 2s. 6d.; half-roxburgh, 4s.
Delectable Duchy, The. Some Tales of East Cornwall. By Q. 6s.
Dickens, Character Sketches from. FIRST, SECOND, and THIRD SERIES. With Six Original Drawings in each by F. BARNARD. 21s. each.
Dick Whittington, A Modern. By JAMES PAYN. In One Vol., 6s.
Dog, Illustrated Book of the. By VERO SHAW, B.A. With 28 Coloured Plates. Cloth bevelled, 35s.; half-morocco, 45s.
Domestic Dictionary, The. Illustrated. Cloth, 7s. 6d.
Doré Bible, The. With 200 Full-page Illustrations by DORÉ. 15s.
Doré Don Quixote, The. With about 400 Illustrations by GUSTAVE DORÉ. *Cheap Edition.* Bevelled boards, gilt edges, 10s. 6d.
Doré Gallery, The. With 250 Illustrations by DORÉ. 4to, 42s.
Doré's Dante's Inferno. Illustrated by GUSTAVE DORÉ. With Preface by A. J. BUTLER. Cloth gilt or buckram, 7s. 6d.
Doré's Dante's Purgatory and Paradise. Illustrated by GUSTAVE DORÉ. *Cheap Edition.* 7s. 6d.
Doré's Milton's Paradise Lost. Illustrated by DORÉ. 4to, 21s.
Dorset, Old. Chapters in the History of the County. By H. J. MOULE, M.A. 10s. 6d.
Dr. Dumány's Wife. A Novel. By MAURUS JÓKAI. 6s.

Selections from Cassell & Company's Publications.

Dulce Domum. Rhymes and Songs for Children. Edited by JOHN FARMER, Editor of "Gaudeamus," &c. Old Notation and Words, 5s. N.B.—The words of the Songs in "Dulce Domum" (with the Airs both in Tonic Sol-fa and Old Notation) can be had in Two Parts, 6d. each.
Earth, Our, and its Story. By Dr. ROBERT BROWN, F.L.S. With Coloured Plates and numerous Wood Engravings. Three Vols. 9s. each.
Edinburgh, Old and New. With 600 Illustrations. Three Vols. 9s. each.
Egypt: Descriptive, Historical, and Picturesque. By Prof. G. EBERS. With 800 Original Engravings. *Popular Edition.* In Two Vols. 42s.
Electricity in the Service of Man. Illustrated. *New and Revised Edition.* 10s. 6d.
Electricity, Practical. By Prof. W. E. AYRTON. 7s. 6d.
Encyclopædic Dictionary, The. In Fourteen Divisional Vols., 10s. 6d. each; or Seven Vols., half-morocco, 21s. each; half-russia, 25s.
England, Cassell's Illustrated History of. With 2,000 Illustrations. Ten Vols., 4to, 9s. each. *Revised Edition.* Vols. I. to VI. 9s. each.
English Dictionary, Cassell's. Giving definitions of more than 100,000 Words and Phrases. Cloth, 7s. 6d. *Cheap Edition.* 3s. 6d.
English History, The Dictionary of. *Cheap Edition.* 10s. 6d.
English Literature, Library of. By Prof. HENRY MORLEY. Complete in Five Vols., 7s. 6d. each.
English Literature, Morley's First Sketch of. *Revised Edition.* 7s. 6d.
English Literature, The Story of. By ANNA BUCKLAND. 3s. 6d.
English Writers. By Prof. HENRY MORLEY. Vols. I. to X. 5s. each.
Etiquette of Good Society. *New Edition.* Edited and Revised by LADY COLIN CAMPBELL. 1s.; cloth, 1s. 6d.
Fairway Island. By HORACE HUTCHINSON. With 4 Full-page Plates. *Cheap Edition.* 3s. 6d.
Faith Doctor, The. A Novel. By Dr. EDWARD EGGLESTON. 6s.
Family Physician, The. By Eminent PHYSICIANS and SURGEONS. *New and Revised Edition.* Cloth, 21s.; Roxburgh, 25s.
Father Stafford. A Novel. By ANTHONY HOPE. 6s.
Field Naturalist's Handbook, The. By the Revs. J. G. WOOD and THEODORE WOOD. *Cheap Edition.* 2s. 6d.
Figuier's Popular Scientific Works. With Several Hundred Illustrations in each. Newly Revised and Corrected. 3s. 6d. each.
  THE HUMAN RACE.   MAMMALIA.   OCEAN WORLD.
      THE INSECT WORLD.   REPTILES AND BIRDS.
  WORLD BEFORE THE DELUGE. THE VEGETABLE WORLD.
Flora's Feast. A Masque of Flowers. Penned and Pictured by WALTER CRANE. With 40 Pages in Colours. 5s.
Football, The Rugby Union Game. Edited by REV. F. MARSHALL. Illustrated. 7s. 6d.
Fraser, John Drummond. By PHILALETHES. A Story of Jesuit Intrigue in the Church of England. 5s.
Garden Flowers, Familiar. By SHIRLEY HIBBERD. With Coloured Plates by F. E. HULME, F.L.S. Complete in Five Series. 12s. 6d. each.
Gardening, Cassell's Popular. Illustrated. Four Vols. 5s. each.
George Saxon, The Reputation of. By MORLEY ROBERTS. 5s.
Gleanings from Popular Authors. Two Vols. With Original Illustrations. 4to, 9s. each. Two Vols. in One, 15s.
Gulliver's Travels. With 88 Engravings by MORTEN. *Cheap Edition.* Cloth, 3s. 6d.; cloth gilt, 5s.
Gun and its Development, The. By W. W. GREENER. With 500 Illustrations. 10s. 6d.

Selections from Cassell & Company's Publications.

Heavens, The Story of the. By Sir ROBERT STAWELL BALL, LL.D., F.R.S., F.R.A.S. With Coloured Plates. *Popular Edition.* 12s. 6d.
Heroes of Britain in Peace and War. With 300 Original Illustrations. Two Vols., 3s. 6d. each; or One Vol., 7s. 6d.
Historic Houses of the United Kingdom. Profusely Illustrated. 10s. 6d.
History, A Foot-note to. Eight Years of Trouble in Samoa. By ROBERT LOUIS STEVENSON. 6s.
Home Life of the Ancient Greeks, The. Translated by ALICE ZIMMERN. Illustrated. 7s. 6d.
Horse, The Book of the. By SAMUEL SIDNEY. Thoroughly Revised and brought up to date by JAMES SINCLAIR and W. C. A. BLEW. With 17 Full-page Collotype Plates of Celebrated Horses of the Day, and numerous other Illustrations. Cloth, 15s.
Houghton, Lord : The Life, Letters, and Friendships of Richard Monckton Milnes, First Lord Houghton. By T. WEMYSS REID. In Two Vols., with Two Portraits. 32s.
Household, Cassell's Book of the. Complete in Four Vols. 5s. each. Four Vols. in Two, half-morocco, 25s.
Hygiene and Public Health. By B. ARTHUR WHITELEGGE, M.D. 7s. 6d.
India, Cassell's History of. By JAMES GRANT. With about 400 Illustrations. Two Vols., 9s. each. One Vol., 15s.
In-door Amusements, Card Games, and Fireside Fun, Cassell's Book of. *Cheap Edition.* 2s.
Into the Unknown: A Romance of South Africa. By LAWRENCE FLETCHER. 4s.
Iron Pirate, The. A Plain Tale of Strange Happenings on the Sea. By MAX PEMBERTON. Illustrated. 5s.
Island Nights' Entertainments. By R. L. STEVENSON. Illustrated. 6s.
Italy from the Fall of Napoleon I. in 1815 to 1890. By J. W. PROBYN. *New and Cheaper Edition.* 3s. 6d.
Joy and Health. By MARTELLIUS. 3s. 6d. *Édition de Luxe*, 7s. 6d.
Kennel Guide, The Practical. By Dr. GORDON STABLES. 1s.
King's Hussar, A. By HERBERT COMPTON. 6s.
"La Bella," and Others. Being Certain Stories Recollected by Egerton Castle, Author of "Consequences." 6s.
Ladies' Physician, The. By a London Physician. 6s.
Lady's Dressing-room, The. Translated from the French of BARONESS STAFFE by LADY COLIN CAMPBELL. 3s. 6d.
Leona. By Mrs. MOLESWORTH. 6s.
Letters, the Highway of, and its Echoes of Famous Footsteps. By THOMAS ARCHER. Illustrated. 10s. 6d.
Letts's Diaries and other Time-saving Publications published exclusively by CASSELL & COMPANY. (*A list free on application.*)
'Lisbeth. By LESLIE KEITH. Three Volumes. 31s. 6d.
List, ye Landsmen! A Romance of Incident. By W. CLARK RUSSELL. *Cheap Edition*, in One Vol., 6s.
Little Minister, The. By J. M. BARRIE. *Illustrated Edition.* 6s.
Little Squire, The. A Story of Three. By Mrs. HENRY DE LA PASTURE. 3s. 6d.
Locomotive Engine, The Biography of a. By HENRY FRITH. 5s.
Loftus, Lord Augustus, The Diplomatic Reminiscences of. First and Second Series. Two Vols., each with Portrait, 32s. each Series.
London, Greater. By EDWARD WALFORD. Two Vols. With about 400 Illustrations. 9s. each.
London, Old and New. Six Vols., each containing about 200 Illustrations and Maps. Cloth, 9s. each.
London Street Arabs. By Mrs. H. M. STANLEY. Illustrated, 5s.
Medicine Lady, The. By L. T. MEADE. In One Vol., 6s.
Medicine, Manuals for Students of. (*A List forwarded post free.*)

Selections from Cassell & Company's Publications.

Modern Europe, A History of. By C. A. FYFFE, M.A. Complete in Three Vols., with full-page Illustrations, 7s. 6d. each.
Mount Desolation. An Australian Romance. By W. CARLTON DAWE. 5s.
Music, Illustrated History of. By EMIL NAUMANN. Edited by the Rev. Sir F. A. GORE OUSELEY, Bart. Illustrated. Two Vols. 31s. 6d.
Musical and Dramatic Copyright, The Law of. By EDWARD CUTLER, THOMAS EUSTACE SMITH, and FREDERIC E. WEATHERLY, Barristers-at-Law. 3s. 6d.
Napier, Life and Letters of the Rt. Hon. Sir Joseph, Bart., LL.D., &c. By A. C. EWALD, F.S.A. *New and Revised Edition.* 7s. 6d.
National Library, Cassell's. In Volumes. Paper covers, 3d.; cloth, 6d. (*A Complete List of the Volumes post free on application.*)
Natural History, Cassell's Concise. By E. PERCEVAL WRIGHT, M.A., M.D., F.L.S. With several Hundred Illustrations. 7s. 6d.
Natural History, Cassell's New. Edited by Prof. P. MARTIN DUNCAN, M.B., F.R.S., F.G.S. Complete in Six Vols. With about 2,000 Illustrations. Cloth, 9s. each.
Nature's Wonder Workers. By KATE R. LOVELL. Illustrated. 3s. 6d.
New England Boyhood, A. By EDWARD E. HALE. 3s. 6d.
Nursing for the Home and for the Hospital, A Handbook of. By CATHERINE J. WOOD. *Cheap Edition.* 1s. 6d.; cloth, 2s.
Nursing of Sick Children, A Handbook for the. By CATHERINE J. WOOD. 2s. 6d.
O'Driscoll's Weird, and other Stories. By A. WERNER. 5s.
Odyssey, The Modern; or, Ulysses up to Date. Cloth gilt, 10s. 6d.
Ohio, The New. A Story of East and West. By EDWARD E. HALE. 6s.
Oil Painting, A Manual of. By the Hon. JOHN COLLIER. 2s. 6d.
Our Own Country. Six Vols. With 1,200 Illustrations. 7s. 6d. each.
Out of the Jaws of Death. By FRANK BARRETT. In One Vol., 6s.
Painting, The English School of. *Cheap Edition.* 3s. 6d.
Painting, Practical Guides to. With Coloured Plates:—

MARINE PAINTING. 5s.	TREE PAINTING. 5s.
ANIMAL PAINTING. 5s.	WATER-COLOUR PAINTING. 5s.
CHINA PAINTING. 5s.	NEUTRAL TINT. 5s.
FIGURE PAINTING. 7s. 6d.	SEPIA, in Two Vols., 3s. each; or in One Vol., 5s.
ELEMENTARY FLOWER PAINTING. 3s.	FLOWERS, AND HOW TO PAINT THEM. 5s.

Paris, Old and New. A Narrative of its History, its People, and its Places. By H. SUTHERLAND EDWARDS. Profusely Illustrated. Vol. I., 9s.; or gilt edges, 10s. 6d.
Peoples of the World, The. In Six Vols. By Dr. ROBERT BROWN. Illustrated. 7s. 6d. each.
Perfect Gentleman, The. By the Rev. A. SMYTHE-PALMER, D.D. 3s. 6d.
Photography for Amateurs. By T. C. HEPWORTH. *Enlarged and Revised Edition.* Illustrated. 1s.; or cloth, 1s. 6d.
Phrase and Fable, Dictionary of. By the Rev. Dr. BREWER. *Cheap Edition, Enlarged*, cloth, 3s. 6d.; or with leather back, 4s. 6d.
Picturesque America. Complete in Four Vols., with 48 Exquisite Steel Plates and about 800 Original Wood Engravings. £2 2s. each.
Picturesque Canada. With 600 Original Illustrations. Two Vols. £6 6s. the Set.
Picturesque Europe. Complete in Five Vols. Each containing 13 Exquisite Steel Plates, from Original Drawings, and nearly 200 Original Illustrations. Cloth, £21; half-morocco, £31 10s.; morocco gilt, £52 10s. POPULAR EDITION. In Five Vols., 18s. each.
Picturesque Mediterranean, The. With Magnificent Original Illustrations by the leading Artists of the Day. Complete in Two Vols. £2 2s. each.
Pigeon Keeper, The Practical. By LEWIS WRIGHT. Illustrated. 3s. 6d.
Pigeons, The Book of. By ROBERT FULTON. Edited and Arranged by L. WRIGHT. With 50 Coloured Plates, 31s. 6d.; half-morocco, £2 2s.

Selections from Cassell & Company's Publications.

Pity and of Death, The Book of. By PIERRE LOTI. Translated by T. P. O'CONNOR, M.P. 5s.
Planet, The Story of Our. By T. G. BONNEY, D.Sc., LL.D., F.R.S., F.S.A., F.G.S. With Six Coloured Plates and Maps and about 100 Illustrations. 31s. 6d.
Playthings and Parodies. Short Stories by BARRY PAIN. 5s.
Poems, Aubrey de Vere's. A Selection. Edited by J. DENNIS. 3s. 6d.
Poetry, The Nature and Elements of. By E. C. STEDMAN. 6s.
Poets, Cassell's Miniature Library of the. Price 1s. each Vol.
Portrait Gallery, The Cabinet. First, Second, Third, and Fourth Series, each containing 36 Cabinet Photographs of Eminent Men and Women. With Biographical Sketches. 15s. each.
Poultry Keeper, The Practical. By L. WRIGHT. Illustrated. 3s. 6d.
Poultry, The Book of. By LEWIS WRIGHT. *Popular Edition.* 10s. 6d.
Poultry, The Illustrated Book of. By LEWIS WRIGHT. With Fifty Coloured Plates. *New and Revised Edition.* Cloth, 31s. 6d.
Prison Princess, A. A Romance of Millbank Penitentiary. By Major ARTHUR GRIFFITHS. 6s.
Q's Works, Uniform Edition of. 5s. each.
Dead Man's Rock. | The Astonishing History of Troy Town.
The Splendid Spur. | "I Saw Three Ships," and other Winter's Tales
The Blue Pavilions. | Noughts and Crosses.
Queen Summer; or, The Tourney of the Lily and the Rose. With Forty Pages of Designs in Colours by WALTER CRANE. 6s.
Queen Victoria, The Life and Times of. By ROBERT WILSON. Complete in Two Vols. With numerous Illustrations. 9s. each.
Quickening of Caliban, The. A Modern Story of Evolution. By J. COMPTON RICKETT. 5s.
Rabbit-Keeper, The Practical. By CUNICULUS. Illustrated. 3s. 6d.
Raffles Haw, The Doings of. By A. CONAN DOYLE. *New Edition.* 5s.
Railways, Our. Their Development, Enterprise, Incident, and Romance. By JOHN PENDLETON. Illustrated. 2 Vols., demy 8vo, 24s.
Railway Guides, Official Illustrated. With Illustrations, Maps, &c. Price 1s. each; or in cloth, 2s. each.

GREAT EASTERN RAILWAY.	GREAT WESTERN RAILWAY.
GREAT NORTHERN RAILWAY.	LONDON AND SOUTH-WESTERN RAILWAY.
LONDON, BRIGHTON AND SOUTH COAST RAILWAY.	MIDLAND RAILWAY.
LONDON AND NORTH-WESTERN RAILWAY.	SOUTH-EASTERN RAILWAY.

Rovings of a Restless Boy, The. By KATHARINE B. FOOT. Illustrated. 5s.
Railway Library, Cassell's. Crown 8vo, boards, 2s. each.

METZEROTT, SHOEMAKER. By KATHARINE P. WOODS.	JACK GORDON, KNIGHT ERRANT, GOTHAM, 1883. By BARCLAY NORTH.
DAVID TODD. By DAVID MACLURE.	THE DIAMOND BUTTON. By BARCLAY NORTH.
THE ADMIRABLE LADY BIDDY FANE. By FRANK BARRETT.	ANOTHER'S CRIME. By JULIAN HAWTHORNE.
COMMODORE JUNK. By G. MANVILLE FENN.	THE YOKE OF THE THORAH. By SIDNEY LUSKA.
ST. CUTHBERT'S TOWER. By FLORENCE WARDEN.	WHO IS JOHN NOMAN? By CHARLES HENRY BECKETT.
THE MAN WITH A THUMB. By BARCLAY NORTH.	THE TRAGEDY OF BRINKWATER. By MARTHA L. MOODEY.
BY RIGHT NOT LAW. By R. SHERARD.	AN AMERICAN PENMAN. By JULIAN HAWTHORNE.
WITHIN SOUND OF THE WEIR. By THOMAS ST. E. HAKE.	SECTION 558; or, THE FATAL LETTER. By JULIAN HAWTHORNE.
UNDER A STRANGE MASK. By FRANK BARRETT.	THE BROWN STONE BOY. By W. H. BISHOP.
THE COOMBSBERROW MYSTERY. By JAMES COLWALL.	A TRAGIC MYSTERY. By JULIAN HAWTHORNE.
A QUEER RACE. By W. WESTALL.	THE GREAT BANK ROBBERY. By JULIAN HAWTHORNE.
CAPTAIN TRAFALGAR. By WESTALL and LAURIE.	
THE PHANTOM CITY. By W. WESTALL.	

Selections from Cassell & Company's Publications.

Rivers of Great Britain: Descriptive, Historical, Pictorial.
   THE ROYAL RIVER: The Thames, from Source to Sea. *Popular Edition*, 16s.
   RIVERS OF THE EAST COAST. With highly finished Engravings. *Popular Edition*, 16s.
Robinson Crusoe, Cassell's New Fine-Art Edition of. With upwards of 100 Original Illustrations. 7s. 6d.
Romance, The World of. Illustrated. Cloth, 9s.
Russo-Turkish War, Cassell's History of. With about 500 Illustrations. Two Vols. 9s. each.
Salisbury Parliament, A Diary of the. By H. W. LUCY. Illustrated by HARRY FURNISS. 21s.
Saturday Journal, Cassell's. Yearly Volume, cloth, 7s. 6d.
Scarabæus. The Story of an African Beetle. By the MARQUISE CLARA LANZA and JAMES CLARENCE HARVEY. *Cheap Edition.* 3s. 6d.
Science for All. Edited by Dr. ROBERT BROWN. *Revised Edition.* Illustrated. Five Vols. 9s. each.
Shadow of a Song, The. A Novel. By CECIL HARLEY. 5s.
Shaftesbury, The Seventh Earl of, K.G., The Life and Work of. By EDWIN HODDER. *Cheap Edition.* 3s. 6d.
Shakespeare, The Plays of. Edited by Professor HENRY MORLEY. Complete in Thirteen Vols., cloth, 21s.; half-morocco, cloth sides, 42s.
Shakespeare, Cassell's Quarto Edition. Containing about 600 Illustrations by H. C. SELOUS. Complete in Three Vols., cloth gilt, £3 3s.
Shakespeare, Miniature. Illustrated. In Twelve Vols., in box, 12s.; or in Red Paste Grain (box to match), with spring catch, 21s.
Shakspere, The International. *Édition de Luxe.*
   "King Henry VIII." Illustrated by SIR JAMES LINTON, P.R.I. (*Price on application.*)
   "Othello." Illustrated by FRANK DICKSEE, R.A. £3 10s.
   "King Henry IV." Illustrated by EDUARD GRÜTZNER. £3 10s.
   "As You Like It." Illustrated by ÉMILE BAYARD. £3 10s.
   "Romeo and Juliet." Illustrated by F. DICKSEE, R.A. Is now out of print, and scarce.
Shakspere, The Leopold. With 400 Illustrations. *Cheap Edition.* 3s. 6d. Cloth gilt, gilt edges, 5s.; Roxburgh, 7s. 6d.
Shakspere, The Royal. With Steel Plates and Wood Engravings. Three Vols. 15s. each.
Sketches, The Art of Making and Using. From the French of G. FRAIPONT. By CLARA BELL. With 50 Illustrations. 2s. 6d.
Smuggling Days and Smuggling Ways. By Commander the Hon. HENRY N. SHORE, R.N. With numerous Illustrations. 7s. 6d.
Snare of the Fowler, The. By Mrs. ALEXANDER. In One Vol., 6s.
Social Welfare, Subjects of. By Rt. Hon. LORD PLAYFAIR, K.C.B. 7s.6d.
Social England. A Record of the Progress of the people in Religion, Laws, Learning, Arts, Science, Literature, and Manners, from the Earliest Times to the Present Day. By various writers. Edited by H. D. TRAILL, D.C.L. Vol. I.—From the Earliest Times to the Accession of Edward the First. 15s.
Sports and Pastimes, Cassell's Complete Book of. *Cheap Edition.* With more than 900 Illustrations. Medium 8vo, 992 pages, cloth, 3s. 6d.
Squire, The. By Mrs. PARR. In One Vol., 6s.
Star-Land. By Sir R. S. BALL, LL.D., &c. Illustrated. 6s.
Storehouse of General Information, Cassell's. With Wood Engravings, Maps, and Coloured Plates. In Vols., 5s. each.
Story of Francis Cludde, The. By STANLEY J. WEYMAN. 6s.
Story Poems. For Young and Old. Edited by E. DAVENPORT. 3s. 6d.
Successful Life, The. By AN ELDER BROTHER. 3s. 6d.

Selections from Cassell & Company's Publications.

Sun, The. By Sir ROBERT STAWELL BALL, LL.D., F.R.S., F.R.A.S. Illustrated with Eight Coloured Plates. 21s.
Sunshine Series, Cassell's. Monthly Volumes. 1s. each.

The Temptation of Dulce Carruthers. By C. E. C. WEIGALL.	On Stronger Wings. By EDITH LISTER.
Lady Lorrimer's Scheme and The Story of a Glamour. By EDITH E. CUTHELL.	You'll Love Me Yet. By FRANCES HASWELL; and That Little Woman. By IDA LEMON.
Womanlike. By FLORENCE M. KING.	

Sybil Knox: a Story of To-day. By EDWARD E. HALE. 6s.
Thackeray, Character Sketches from. Six New and Original Drawings by FREDERICK BARNARD, reproduced in Photogravure. 21s.
Thackeray in America, With. By EYRE CROWE, A.R.A. Illustrated. 10s. 6d.
The "Short Story" Library.

Otto the Knight, &c. By OCTAVE THANET. 5s.	Eleven Possible Cases. By Various Authors. 6s.
Fourteen to One, &c. By ELIZABETH STUART PHELPS. 5s.	Felicia. By Miss FANNY MURFREE. 5s. The Poet's Audience, and Delilah. By CLARA SAVILE CLARKE. 5s.

The "Treasure Island" Series. *Cheap Illustrated Editions.* Cloth, 3s. 6d. each.

"Kidnapped." By R. L. STEVENSON.	The Black Arrow. By ROBERT LOUIS STEVENSON.
Treasure Island. By ROBERT LOUIS STEVENSON.	
The Master of Ballantrae. By ROBERT LOUIS STEVENSON.	King Solomon's Mines. By H. RIDER HAGGARD.

Tiny Luttrell. By E. W. HORNUNG. Cloth gilt, Two Vols. 21s.
Trees, Familiar. By G. S. BOULGER, F.L.S. Two Series. With 40 full-page Coloured Plates by W. H. J. BOOT. 12s. 6d. each.
"Unicode": the Universal Telegraphic Phrase Book. *Desk or Pocket Edition.* 2s. 6d.
United States, Cassell's History of the. By EDMUND OLLIER. With 600 Illustrations. Three Vols. 9s. each.
Universal History, Cassell's Illustrated. Four Vols. 9s. each.
Wild Birds, Familiar. By W. SWAYSLAND. Four Series. With 40 Coloured Plates in each. 12s. 6d. each.
Wild Flowers, Familiar. By F. E. HULME, F.L.S., F.S.A. Five Series. With 40 Coloured Plates in each. 12s. 6d. each.
Won at the Last Hole. A Golfing Romance. By M. A. STOBART. Illustrated. 1s. 6d.
Wood, Rev. J. G., Life of the. By the Rev. THEODORE WOOD. Extra crown 8vo, cloth. *Cheap Edition.* 5s.
Work. The Illustrated Journal for Mechanics. *New and Enlarged Series.* Vols. V. and VI., 4s. each.
World of Wit and Humour, The. With 400 Illustrations. 7s. 6d.
World of Wonders. Two Vols. With 400 Illustrations. 7s. 6d. each.
Wrecker, The. By R. L. STEVENSON and L. OSBOURNE. Illustrated. 6s.
Yule Tide. Cassell's Christmas Annual. 1s.

ILLUSTRATED MAGAZINES.

The Quiver. ENLARGED SERIES. Monthly, 6d.
Cassell's Family Magazine. Monthly, 7d.
"Little Folks" Magazine. Monthly, 6d.
The Magazine of Art. Monthly, 1s.
"Chums." Illustrated Paper for Boys. Weekly, 1d.; Monthly, 6d.
Cassell's Saturday Journal. Weekly, 1d.; Monthly, 6d.
Work. Weekly, 1d.; Monthly, 6d.

CASSELL'S COMPLETE CATALOGUE, containing particulars of upwards of One Thousand Volumes, will be sent post free on application.

CASSELL & COMPANY, LIMITED, *Ludgate Hill, London.*

Selections from Cassell & Company's Publications.

Bibles and Religious Works.

Bible Biographies. Illustrated. 2s. 6d. each.
The Story of Moses and Joshua. By the Rev. J. TELFORD.
The Story of the Judges. By the Rev. J. WYCLIFFE GEDGE.
The Story of Samuel and Saul. By the Rev. D. C. TOVEY.
The Story of David. By the Rev. J. WILD.
The Story of Joseph. Its Lessons for To-Day. By the Rev. GEORGE BAINTON.

The Story of Jesus. In Verse. By J. R. MACDUFF, D.D.
Bible, Cassell's Illustrated Family. With 900 Illustrations. Leather, gilt edges, £2 10s.
Bible Educator, The. Edited by the Very Rev. Dean PLUMPTRE, D.D., With Illustrations, Maps, &c. Four Vols., cloth, 6s. each.
Bible Student in the British Museum, The. By the Rev. J. G. KITCHIN, M.A. *New and Revised Edition.* 1s. 4d.
Biblewomen and Nurses. Yearly Volume. Illustrated. 3s.
Bunyan's Pilgrim's Progress. Illustrated throughout. Cloth, 3s. 6d.; cloth gilt, gilt edges, 5s.
Child's Bible, The. With 200 Illustrations. 150th *Thousand.* 7s. 6d.
Child's Life of Christ, The. With 200 Illustrations. 7s. 6d.
"Come, ye Children." Illustrated. By Rev. BENJAMIN WAUGH. 5s.
Conquests of the Cross. Illustrated. In 3 Vols. 9s. each.
Doré Bible. With 238 Illustrations by GUSTAVE DORÉ. Small folio, best morocco, gilt edges, £15. *Popular Edition.* With 200 Illustrations. 15s.
Early Days of Christianity, The. By the Ven. Archdeacon FARRAR, D.D., F.R.S. LIBRARY EDITION. Two Vols., 24s.; morocco, £2 2s. POPULAR EDITION. Complete in One Volume, cloth, 6s.; cloth, gilt edges, 7s. 6d.; Persian morocco, 10s. 6d.; tree-calf, 15s.
Family Prayer-Book, The. Edited by Rev. Canon GARBETT, M.A., and Rev. S. MARTIN. Extra crown 4to, cloth, 5s.; morocco, 18s.
Gleanings after Harvest. Studies and Sketches by the Rev. JOHN R. VERNON, M.A. Illustrated. 6s.
"Graven in the Rock." By the Rev. Dr. SAMUEL KINNS, F.R.A.S., Author of "Moses and Geology." Illustrated. 12s. 6d.
"Heart Chords." A Series of Works by Eminent Divines. Bound in cloth, red edges, One Shilling each.

MY BIBLE. By the Right Rev. W. BOYD CARPENTER, Bishop of Ripon.
MY FATHER. By the Right Rev. ASHTON OXENDEN, late Bishop of Montreal.
MY WORK FOR GOD. By the Right Rev. Bishop COTTERILL.
MY OBJECT IN LIFE. By the Ven. Archdeacon FARRAR, D.D.
MY ASPIRATIONS. By the Rev. G. MATHESON, D.D.
MY EMOTIONAL LIFE. By the Rev. Preb. CHADWICK, D.D.
MY BODY. By the Rev. Prof. W. G. BLAIKIE, D.D.

MY GROWTH IN DIVINE LIFE. By the Rev. Preb. REYNOLDS, M.A.
MY SOUL. By the Rev. P. B. POWER, M.A.
MY HEREAFTER. By the Very Rev. Dean BICKERSTETH.
MY WALK WITH GOD. By the Very Rev. Dean MONTGOMERY.
MY AIDS TO THE DIVINE LIFE. By the Very Rev. Dean BOYLE.
MY SOURCES OF STRENGTH. By the Rev. E. E. JENKINS, M.A., Secretary of Wesleyan Missionary Society.

Helps to Belief. A Series of Helpful Manuals on the Religious Difficulties of the Day. Edited by the Rev. TEIGNMOUTH SHORE, M.A., Canon of Worcester. Cloth, 1s. each.

CREATION. By Dr. H. Goodwin, the late Lord Bishop of Carlisle.
THE DIVINITY OF OUR LORD. By the Lord Bishop of Derry.
THE MORALITY OF THE OLD TESTAMENT. By the Rev. Newman Smyth, D.D.

MIRACLES. By the Rev. Brownlow Maitland, M.A.
PRAYER. By the Rev. T. Teignmouth Shore, M.A.
THE ATONEMENT. By William Conner Magee, D.D., Late Archbishop of York.

Holy Land and the Bible, The. By the Rev. C. GEIKIE, D.D., LL.D. (Edin.). Two Vols., 24s. *Illustrated Edition*, One Vol., 21s.

5 B. 11.93

Selections from Cassell & Company's Publications.

Lectures on Christianity and Socialism. By the Right Rev. ALFRED BARRY, D.D. Cloth, 3s. 6d.

Life of Christ, The. By the Ven. Archdeacon FARRAR, D.D., F.R.S. LIBRARY EDITION. Two Vols. Cloth, 24s.; morocco, 42s. CHEAP ILLUSTRATED EDITION. Cloth, 7s. 6d.; cloth, full gilt, gilt edges, 10s. 6d. POPULAR EDITION, in One Vol., 8vo, cloth, 6s.; cloth, gilt edges, 7s. 6d.; Persian morocco, gilt edges, 10s. 6d.; tree-calf, 15s.

Moses and Geology; or, The Harmony of the Bible with Science. By the Rev. SAMUEL KINNS, Ph.D., F.R.A.S. Illustrated. *New Edition* on Larger and Superior Paper. 8s. 6d.

New Light on the Bible and the Holy Land. By B. T. A. EVETTS, M.A. Illustrated. 21s.

New Testament Commentary for English Readers, The. Edited by the Rt. Rev. C. J. ELLICOTT, D.D., Lord Bishop of Gloucester and Bristol. In Three Volumes. 21s. each. Vol. I.—The Four Gospels. Vol. II.—The Acts, Romans, Corinthians, Galatians. Vol. III.—The remaining Books of the New Testament.

New Testament Commentary. Edited by Bishop ELLICOTT. Handy Volume Edition. St. Matthew, 3s. 6d. St. Mark, 3s. St. Luke, 3s. 6d. St. John, 3s. 6d. The Acts of the Apostles, 3s. 6d. Romans, 2s. 6d. Corinthians I. and II., 3s. Galatians, Ephesians, and Philippians, 3s. Colossians, Thessalonians, and Timothy, 3s. Titus, Philemon, Hebrews, and James, 3s. Peter, Jude, and John, 3s. The Revelation, 3s. An Introduction to the New Testament, 3s. 6d.

Old Testament Commentary for English Readers, The. Edited by the Right Rev. C. J. ELLICOTT, D.D., Lord Bishop of Gloucester and Bristol. Complete in Five Vols. 21s. each. Vol. I.—Genesis to Numbers. Vol. II.—Deuteronomy to Samuel II. Vol. III.—Kings I. to Esther. Vol. IV.—Job to Isaiah. Vol. V.—Jeremiah to Malachi.

Old Testament Commentary. Edited by Bishop ELLICOTT. Handy Volume Edition. Genesis, 3s. 6d. Exodus, 3s. Leviticus, 3s. Numbers, 2s. 6d. Deuteronomy, 2s. 6d.

Old and New Testaments, Plain Introductions to the Books of the. Containing Contributions by many Eminent Divines. In Two Volumes, 3s. 6d. each.

Protestantism, The History of. By the Rev. J. A. WYLIE, LL.D. Containing upwards of 600 Original Illustrations. Three Vols. 9s. each.

Quiver Yearly Volume, The. With about 600 Original Illustrations. 7s. 6d.

Religion, The Dictionary of. By the Rev. W. BENHAM, B.D. *Cheap Edition.* 10s. 6d.

St. George for England; and other Sermons preached to Children. By the Rev. T. TEIGNMOUTH SHORE, M.A., Canon of Worcester. 5s.

St. Paul, The Life and Work of. By the Ven. Archdeacon FARRAR, D.D., F.R.S., Chaplain-in-Ordinary to the Queen. LIBRARY EDITION. Two Vols., cloth, 24s.; calf, 42s. ILLUSTRATED EDITION, complete in One Volume, with about 300 Illustrations, £1 1s.; morocco, £2 2s. POPULAR EDITION. One Volume, 8vo, cloth, 6s.; cloth, gilt edges, 7s. 6d.; Persian morocco, 10s. 6d.; tree-calf, 15s.

Shall We Know One Another in Heaven? By the Rt. Rev. J. C. RYLE, D.D., Bishop of Liverpool. *Cheap Edition.* Paper covers, 6d.

Signa Christi. By the Rev. JAMES AITCHISON. 5s.

"Sunday," Its Origin, History, and Present Obligation. By the Ven. Archdeacon HESSEY, D.C.L. *Fifth Edition.* 7s. 6d.

Twilight of Life, The. Words of Counsel and Comfort for the Aged. By the Rev. JOHN ELLERTON, M.A. 1s. 6d.

Selections from Cassell & Company's Publications.

Educational Works and Students' Manuals.

Agricultural Text-Books, Cassell's. (The "Downton" Series.) Edited by JOHN WRIGHTSON, Professor of Agriculture. Fully Illustrated, 2s. 6d. each.—Farm Crops. By Prof. WRIGHTSON.—Soils and Manures. By J. M. H. MUNRO, D.Sc. (London), F.I.C., F.C.S. —Live Stock. By Prof. WRIGHTSON.
Alphabet, Cassell's Pictorial. 3s. 6d.
Arithmetics, The Modern School. By GEORGE RICKS, B.Sc. Lond. With Test Cards. (*List on application.*)
Atlas, Cassell's Popular. Containing 24 Coloured Maps. 2s. 6d.
Book-Keeping. By THEODORE JONES. For Schools, 2s.; cloth, 3s. For the Million, 2s.; cloth, 3s. Books for Jones's System, 2s.
British Empire Map of the World. New Map for Schools and Institutes. By G. R. PARKIN and J. G. BARTHOLOMEW, F.R.G.S. Mounted on cloth, varnished, and with Rollers, or folded. 25s
Chemistry, The Public School. By J. H. ANDERSON, M.A. 2s. 6d.
Cookery for Schools. By LIZZIE HERITAGE. 6d.
Drawing Copies, Cassell's Modern School Freehand. First Grade, 1s.; Second Grade, 2s.
Drawing Copies, Cassell's "New Standard." *Complete in Fourteen Books.* 2d., 3d., and 4d. each.
Energy and Motion. By WILLIAM PAICE, M.A. Illustrated. 1s. 6d.
Euclid, Cassell's. Edited by Prof. WALLACE, M.A. 1s.
Euclid, The First Four Books of. *New Edition.* In paper, 6d.; cloth, 9d.
Experimental Geometry. By PAUL BERT. Illustrated. 1s. 6d.
French, Cassell's Lessons in. *New and Revised Edition.* Parts I. and II., each 2s. 6d.; complete, 4s. 6d. Key, 1s. 6d.
French-English and English-French Dictionary. *Entirely New and Enlarged Edition.* 1,150 pages, 8vo, cloth, 3s. 6d.
French Reader, Cassell's Public School. By G. S. CONRAD. 2s. 6d.
Gaudeamus. Songs for Colleges and Schools. Edited by JOHN FARMER. 5s. Words only, paper covers, 6d.; cloth, 9d.
German Dictionary, Cassell's New (German-English, English-German). *Cheap Edition.* Cloth, 3s. 6d.
Hand-and-Eye Training. By G. RICKS, B.Sc. 2 Vols., with 16 Coloured Plates in each Vol. Cr. 4to, 6s. each. Cards for Class Use, 5 sets, 1s. each.
Historical Cartoons, Cassell's Coloured. Size 45 in. × 35 in., 2s. each. Mounted on canvas and varnished, with rollers, 5s. each.
Historical Course for Schools, Cassell's. Illustrated throughout. I.—Stories from English History, 1s. II.—The Simple Outline of English History, 1s. 3d. III.—The Class History of England, 2s. 6d.
Italian Grammar, The Elements of, with Exercises. Cloth, 3s. 6d.
Latin Dictionary, Cassell's New. (Latin-English and English-Latin.) Revised by J. R. V. MARCHANT, M.A., and J. F. CHARLES, B.A. Cloth, 3s. 6d.
Latin Primer, The First. By Prof. POSTGATE. 1s.
Latin Primer, The New. By Prof. J. P. POSTGATE. Crown 8vo, 2s. 6d.
Latin Prose for Lower Forms. By M. A. BAYFIELD, M.A. 2s. 6d.
Laundry Work (How to Teach It). By Mrs. E. LORD. 6d.
Laws of Every-Day Life. By H. O. ARNOLD-FORSTER, M.P. 1s. 6d. *Special Edition* on Green Paper for Persons with Weak Eyesight. 2s.
Lessons in Our Laws; or, Talks at Broadacre Farm. By H. F. LESTER. Illustrated. Parts I. and II., 1s. 6d. each.
Little Folks' History of England. Illustrated. 1s. 6d.
Making of the Home, The. By Mrs. SAMUEL A. BARNETT. 1s. 6d.
Marlborough Books:—Arithmetic Examples, 3s. French Exercises, 3s. 6d. French Grammar, 2s. 6d. German Grammar, 3s. 6d.
Mechanics and Machine Design, Numerical Examples in Practical. By R. G. BLAINE, M.E. *New Edition, Revised and Enlarged.* With 79 Illustrations. Cloth, 2s. 6d.

Mechanics for Young Beginners, A First Book of. By the Rev. J. G. EASTON, M.A. 4s. 6d.

Natural History Coloured Wall Sheets, Cassell's New. 18 Subjects. Size 39 by 31 in. Mounted on rollers and varnished, 3s. each.

Object Lessons from Nature. By Prof. L. C. MIALL, F.L.S. Fully Illustrated. *New and Enlarged Edition.* Two Vols., 1s. 6d. each.

Physiology for Schools. By A. T. SCHOFIELD, M.D., M.R.C.S., &c. Illustrated. Cloth, 1s. 9d.; Three Parts, paper covers, 5d. each; or cloth limp, 6d. each.

Poetry Readers, Cassell's New. Illustrated. 12 Books, 1d. each; or complete in one Vol., cloth, 1s. 6d.

Popular Educator, Cassell's NEW. With Revised Text, New Maps, New Coloured Plates, New Type, &c. In 8 Vols., 5s. each; or in Four Vols., half-morocco, 50s. the set.

Readers, Cassell's "Higher Class." (*List on application.*)

Readers, Cassell's Readable. Illustrated. (*List on application.*)

Readers for Infant Schools, Coloured. Three Books. 4d. each.

Reader, The Citizen. By H. O. ARNOLD-FORSTER, M.P. Illustrated. 1s. 6d. Also a *Scottish Edition*, cloth, 1s. 6d.

Reader, The Temperance. By Rev. J. DENNIS HIRD. Crown 8vo, 1s. 6d.

Readers, The "Modern School" Geographical. (*List on application.*)

Readers, The "Modern School." Illustrated. (*List on application.*)

Reckoning, Howard's Anglo-American Art of. By C. FRUSHER HOWARD. Paper covers, 1s.; cloth, 2s. *New Edition*, 5s.

Round the Empire. By G. R. PARKIN. Fully Illustrated. 1s. 6d.

Science Applied to Work. By J. A. BOWER. 1s.

Science of Everyday Life. By J. A. BOWER. Illustrated. 1s.

Shade from Models, Common Objects, and Casts of Ornament, How to. By W. E. SPARKES. With 25 Plates by the Author. 3s.

Shakspere's Plays for School Use. 9 Books. Illustrated. 6d. each.

Spelling, A Complete Manual of. By J. D. MORELL, LL.D. 1s.

Technical Manuals, Cassell's. Illustrated throughout :—
Handrailing and Staircasing, 3s. 6d.—Bricklayers, Drawing for, 3s.—Building Construction, 2s. — Cabinet-Makers, Drawing for, 3s. — Carpenters and Joiners, Drawing for, 3s. 6d.—Gothic Stonework, 3s.—Linear Drawing and Practical Geometry, 2s. Linear Drawing and Projection. The Two Vols. in One, 3s. 6d.—Machinists and Engineers, Drawing for, 4s. 6d.—Metal-Plate Workers, Drawing for, 3s.—Model Drawing, 3s.—Orthographical and Isometrical Projection, 2s.—Practical Perspective, 3s.—Stonemasons, Drawing for, 3s.—Applied Mechanics, by Sir R. S. Ball, LL.D., 2s.—Systematic Drawing and Shading, 2s.

Technical Educator, Cassell's NEW. An entirely New Cyclopædia of Technical Education, with Coloured Plates and Engravings. Four Volumes, 5s. each.

Technology, Manuals of. Edited by Prof. AYRTON, F.R.S., and RICHARD WORMELL, D.Sc., M.A. Illustrated throughout :—
The Dyeing of Textile Fabrics, by Prof. Hummel, 5s.—Watch and Clock Making, by D. Glasgow, Vice-President of the British Horological Institute, 4s. 6d.—Steel and Iron, by Prof. W. H. Greenwood, F.C.S., M.I.C.E., &c., 5s.—Spinning Woollen and Worsted, by W. S. B. McLaren, M.P., 4s. 6d.—Design in Textile Fabrics, by T. R. Ashenhurst, 4s. 6d.—Practical Mechanics, by Prof. Perry, M.E., 3s. 6d.—Cutting Tools Worked by Hand and Machine, by Prof. Smith, 3s. 6d.

Things New and Old; or, Stories from English History. By H. O. ARNOLD-FORSTER, M.P. Fully Illustrated, and strongly bound in Cloth. Standards I. & II., 9d. each; Standard III., 1s.; Standard IV., 1s. 3d.; Standards V., VI., & VII., 1s. 6d. each.

This World of Ours. By H. O. ARNOLD-FORSTER, M.P. Illustrated. 3s. 6d.

Selections from Cassell & Company's Publications.

Books for Young People.

"**Little Folks**" **Half-Yearly Volume.** Containing 432 4to pages, with about 200 Illustrations, and Pictures in Colour. Boards, 3s. 6d.; cloth, 5s.

Bo-Peep. A Book for the Little Ones. With Original Stories and Verses. Illustrated throughout. Yearly Volume. Boards, 2s. 6d.; cloth, 3s. 6d.

Beyond the Blue Mountains. By L. T. MEADE. 5s.

The Peep of Day. *Cassell's Illustrated Edition.* 2s. 6d.

Maggie Steele's Diary. By E. A. DILLWYN. 2s. 6d.

A Sunday Story-Book. By MAGGIE BROWNE, SAM BROWNE and AUNT ETHEL. Illustrated. 3s. 6d.

A Bundle of Tales. By MAGGIE BROWNE (Author of "Wanted—a King," &c.), SAM BROWNE, and AUNT ETHEL. 3s. 6d.

Pleasant Work for Busy Fingers. By MAGGIE BROWNE. Illustrated. 5s.

Born a King. By FRANCES and MARY ARNOLD-FORSTER. (The Life of Alfonso XIII., the Boy King of Spain.) Illustrated. 1s.

Cassell's Pictorial Scrap Book. Six Vols. 3s. 6d. each.

Schoolroom and Home Theatricals. By ARTHUR WAUGH. Illustrated. 2s. 6d.

Magic at Home. By Prof. HOFFMAN. Illustrated. Cloth gilt, 5s.

Little Mother Bunch. By Mrs. MOLESWORTH. Illustrated. Cloth, 3s. 6d.

Pictures of School Life and Boyhood. Selected from the best Authors. Edited by PERCY FITZGERALD, M.A. 2s. 6d.

Heroes of Every-day Life. By LAURA LANE. With about 20 Full-page Illustrations. Cloth. 2s. 6d.

Bob Lovell's Career. By EDWARD S. ELLIS. 5s.

Books for Young People. *Cheap Edition.* Illustrated. Cloth gilt, 3s. 6d. each.

The Champion of Odin; or, Viking Life in the Days of Old. By J. Fred. Hodgetts. | Bound by a Spell; or, The Hunted Witch of the Forest. By the Hon. Mrs. Greene.
Under Bayard's Banner. By Henry Frith. |

Books for Young People. Illustrated. 3s. 6d. each.

*Bashful Fifteen. By L. T. Meade.
*The White House at Inch Gow. By Mrs. Pitt.
*A Sweet Girl Graduate. By L. T. Meade.
The King's Command: A Story for Girls. By Maggie Symington.
Lost in Samoa. A Tale of Adventure in the Navigator Islands. By Edward S. Ellis.
Tad; or, "Getting Even" with Him. By Edward S. Ellis.
*The Palace Beautiful. By L. T. Meade.

*Polly: A New-Fashioned Girl. By L. T. Meade.
"Follow My Leader." By Talbot Baines Reed.
*The Cost of a Mistake. By Sarah Pitt.
*A World of Girls: The Story of a School. By L. T. Meade.
Lost among White Africans. By David Ker.
For Fortune and Glory: A Story of the Soudan War. By Lewis Hough.

Also procurable in superior binding, 5s. each.

Crown 8vo Library. *Cheap Editions.* Gilt edges, 2s. 6d. each.

Rambles Round London. By C. L. Matéaux. Illustrated.
Around and About Old England. By C. L. Matéaux. Illustrated.
Paws and Claws. By one of the Authors of "Poems written for a Child." Illustrated.
Decisive Events in History. By Thomas Archer. With Original Illustrations.
The True Robinson Crusoes. Cloth gilt.
Peeps Abroad for Folks at Home. Illustrated throughout.

Wild Adventures in Wild Places. By Dr. Gordon Stables, R.N. Illustrated.
Modern Explorers. By Thomas Frost. Illustrated. *New and Cheaper Edition.*
Early Explorers. By Thomas Frost.
Home Chat with our Young Folks. Illustrated throughout.
Jungle, Peak, and Plain. Illustrated throughout.
The England of Shakespeare. By E. Goadby. With Full-page Illustrations.

Selections from Cassell & Company's Publications.

The "Cross and Crown" Series. Illustrated. 2s. 6d. each.

Freedom's Sword: A Story of the Days of Wallace and Bruce. By Annie S. Swan.
Strong to Suffer: A Story of the Jews. By E. Wynne.
Heroes of the Indian Empire; or, Stories of Valour and Victory. By Ernest Foster.
In Letters of Flame: A Story of the Waldenses. By C. L. Mateaux.
Through Trial to Triumph. By Madeline B. Hunt.
By Fire and Sword: A Story of the Huguenots. By Thomas Archer.
Adam Hepburn's Vow: A Tale of Kirk and Covenant. By Annie S. Swan.
No. XIII.; or, The Story of the Lost Vestal. A Tale of Early Christian Days. By Emma Marshall.

"Golden Mottoes" Series, The. Each Book containing 208 pages, with Four full-page Original Illustrations. Crown 8vo, cloth gilt, 2s. each.

"Nil Desperandum." By the Rev. F. Langbridge, M.A.
"Bear and Forbear." By Sarah Pitt.
"Foremost if I Can." By Helen Atteridge.
"Honour is my Guide." By Jeanie Hering (Mrs. Adams-Acton).
"Aim at a Sure End." By Emily Searchfield.
"He Conquers who Endures." By the Author of "May Cunningham's Trial," &c.

Cassell's Picture Story Books. Each containing about Sixty Pages of Pictures and Stories, &c. 6d. each.

Little Talks.
Bright Stars.
Nursery Toys.
Pet's Posy.
Tiny Tales.
Daisy's Story Book.
Dot's Story Book.
A Nest of Stories.
Good-Night Stories.
Chats for Small Chatterers.
Auntie's Stories.
Birdie's Story Book.
Little Chimes.
A Sheaf of Tales.
Dewdrop Stories.

Cassell's Sixpenny Story Books. All Illustrated, and containing Interesting Stories by well-known writers.

The Smuggler's Cave.
Little Lizzie.
Little Bird, Life and Adventures of.
Luke Barnicott.
The Boat Club.
Little Pickles.
The Elchester College Boys.
My First Cruise.
The Little Peacemaker.
The Delft Jug.

Cassell's Shilling Story Books. All Illustrated, and containing Interesting Stories.

Bunty and the Boys.
The Heir of Elmdale.
The Mystery at Shoncliff School.
Claimed at Last, and Roy's Reward.
Thorns and Tangles.
The Cuckoo in the Robin's Nest.
John's Mistake.
The History of Five Little Pitchers.
Diamonds in the Sand.
Surly Bob.
The Giant's Cradle.
Shag and Doll.
Aunt Lucia's Locket.
The Magic Mirror.
The Cost of Revenge.
Clever Frank.
Among the Redskins.
The Ferryman of Brill.
Harry Maxwell.
A Banished Monarch.
Seventeen Cats.

Illustrated Books for the Little Ones. Containing interesting Stories. All Illustrated. 1s. each; cloth gilt, 1s. 6d.

Tales Told for Sunday.
Sunday Stories for Small People.
Stories and Pictures for Sunday.
Bible Pictures for Boys and Girls.
Firelight Stories.
Sunlight and Shade.
Rub-a-Dub Tales.
Fine Feathers and Fluffy Fur.
Scrambles and Scrapes.
Tittle Tattle Tales.
Up and Down the Garden.
All Sorts of Adventures.
Our Sunday Stories.
Our Holiday Hours.
Indoors and Out.
Some Farm Friends.
Wandering Ways.
Dumb Friends.
Those Golden Sands.
Little Mothers and their Children.
Our Pretty Pets.
Our Schoolday Hours.
Creatures Tame.
Creatures Wild.

Selections from Cassell & Company's Publications.

"Wanted—a King" Series. *Cheap Edition.* Illustrated. 2s. 6d. each.
   Great Grandmamma. By Georgina M. Synge.
   Robin's Ride. By Ellinor Davenport Adams.
   Wanted—a King; or, How Merle set the Nursery Rhymes to Rights. By Maggie Browne. With Original Designs by Harry Furniss.
   Fairy Tales in Other Lands. By Julia Goddard.

The World's Workers. A Series of New and Original Volumes. With Portraits printed on a tint as Frontispiece. 1s. each.
- John Cassell. By G. Holden Pike.
- Charles Haddon Spurgeon. By G. HOLDEN PIKE.
- Dr. Arnold of Rugby. By Rose E. Selfe.
- The Earl of Shaftesbury. By Henry Frith.
- Sarah Robinson, Agnes Weston, and Mrs. Meredith. By E. M. Tomkinson.
- Thomas A. Edison and Samuel F. B. Morse. By Dr. Denslow and J. Marsh Parker.
- Mrs. Somerville and Mary Carpenter. By Phyllis Browne.
- General Gordon. By the Rev. S. A. Swaine.
- Charles Dickens. By his Eldest Daughter.
- Sir Titus Salt and George Moore. By J. Burnley.
- Florence Nightingale, Catherine Marsh, Frances Ridley Havergal, Mrs. Ranyard ("L. N. R."). By Lizzie Alldridge.
- Dr. Guthrie, Father Mathew, Elihu Burritt, George Livesey. By John W. Kirton, LL.D.
- Sir Henry Havelock and Colin Campbell Lord Clyde. By E. C. Phillips.
- Abraham Lincoln. By Ernest Foster.
- George Müller and Andrew Reed. By E. R. Pitman.
- Richard Cobden. By R. Gowing.
- Benjamin Franklin. By E. M. Tomkinson.
- Handel. By Eliza Clarke. [Swaine.
- Turner the Artist. By the Rev. S. A.
- George and Robert Stephenson. By C. L. Matéaux.
- David Livingstone. By Robert Smiles.

⁎⁎⁎ The above Works (excluding RICHARD COBDEN *and* CHARLES HADDON SPURGEON*) can also be had Three in One Vol., cloth, gilt edges,* 3s.

Library of Wonders. Illustrated Gift-books for Boys. Paper, 1s.; cloth, 1s. 6d.
- Wonderful Balloon Ascents
- Wonderful Adventures.
- Wonderful Escapes.
- Wonders of Animal Instinct.
- Wonders of Bodily Strength and Skill.

Cassell's Eighteenpenny Story Books. Illustrated.
- Wee Willie Winkie.
- Ups and Downs of a Donkey's Life.
- Three Wee Ulster Lassies.
- Up the Ladder.
- Dick's Hero; and other Stories.
- The Chip Boy.
- Raggles, Baggles, and the Emperor.
- Roses from Thorns.
- Faith's Father.
- By Land and Sea.
- The Young Berringtons.
- Jeff and Leff.
- Tom Morris's Error.
- Worth more than Gold.
- "Through Flood—Through Fire;" and other Stories.
- The Girl with the Golden Locks.
- Stories of the Olden Time.

Gift Books for Young People. By Popular Authors. With Four Original Illustrations in each. Cloth gilt, 1s. 6d. each.
- The Boy Hunters of Kentucky. By Edward S. Ellis.
- Red Feather: a Tale of the American Frontier. By Edward S. Ellis.
- Seeking a City.
- Rhoda's Reward; or, "If Wishes were Horses."
- Jack Marston's Anchor.
- Frank's Life-Battle; or, The Three Friends.
- Fritters. By Sarah Pitt.
- The Two Hardcastles. By Madeline Bonavia Hunt.
- Major Monk's Motto. By the Rev. F. Langbridge.
- Trixy. By Maggie Symington.
- Rags and Rainbows: A Story of Thanksgiving.
- Uncle William's Charges; or, The Broken Trust.
- Pretty Pink's Purpose; or, The Little Street Merchants.
- Tim Thomson's Trial. By George Weatherly.
- Ursula's Stumbling-Block. By Julia Goddard.
- Ruth's Life-Work. By the Rev. Joseph Johnson.

Cassell's Two-Shilling Story Books. Illustrated.
- Stories of the Tower.
- Mr. Burke's Nieces.
- May Cunningham's Trial.
- The Top of the Ladder: How to Reach it.
- Little Flotsam.
- Madge and Her Friends.
- The Children of the Court.
- Maid Marjory.
- Peggy, and other Tales.
- The Four Cats of the Tippertons.
- Marion's Two Homes.
- Little Folks' Sunday Book.
- Two Fourpenny Bits.
- Poor Nelly.
- Tom Heriot.
- Through Peril to Fortune.
- Aunt Tabitha's Waifs.
- In Mischief Again.

Selections from Cassell & Company's Publications.

Cheap Editions of Popular Volumes for Young People. Bound in cloth, gilt edges, 2s. 6d. each.

In Quest of Gold; or, Under the Whanga Falls.
On Board the *Esmeralda*; or, Martin Leigh's Log.
The Romance of Invention: Vignettes from the Annals of Industry and Science.
For Queen and King.
Esther West.
Three Homes.
Working to Win.
Perils Afloat and Brigands Ashore.

The "Deerfoot" Series. By EDWARD S. ELLIS. With Four full-page Illustrations in each Book. Cloth, bevelled boards, 2s. 6d. each.

The Hunters of the Ozark. | The Camp in the Mountains.
The Last War Trail.

The "Log Cabin" Series. By EDWARD S. ELLIS. With Four Full-page Illustrations in each. Crown 8vo, cloth, 2s. 6d. each.

The Lost Trail. | Camp-Fire and Wigwam.
Footprints in the Forest.

The "Great River" Series. By EDWARD S. ELLIS. Illustrated. Crown 8vo, cloth, bevelled boards, 2s. 6d. each.

Down the Mississippi. | Lost in the Wilds.
Up the Tapajos; or, Adventures in Brazil.

The "Boy Pioneer" Series. By EDWARD S. ELLIS. With Four Full-page Illustrations in each Book. Crown 8vo, cloth, 2s. 6d. each.

Ned in the Woods. A Tale of Early Days in the West.
Ned on the River. A Tale of Indian River Warfare.
Ned in the Block House. A Story of Pioneer Life in Kentucky.

The "World in Pictures." Illustrated throughout. 2s. 6d. each.

A Ramble Round France.
All the Russias.
Chats about Germany.
The Land of the Pyramids (Egypt).
The Eastern Wonderland (Japan).
Glimpses of South America.
Round Africa.
The Land of Temples (India).
The Isles of the Pacific.
Peeps into China.

Half-Crown Story Books.

Margaret's Enemy.
Pen's Perplexities.
Notable Shipwrecks.
At the South Pole.
Soldier and Patriot (George Washington).
The Young Man in the Battle of Life. By the Rev. Dr. Landels.

Books for the Little Ones.

Rhymes for the Young Folk. By William Allingham. Beautifully Illustrated. 3s. 6d.

The History Scrap Book: With nearly 1,000 Engravings: Cloth, 7s. 6d.

My Diary. With 12 Coloured Plates and 366 Woodcuts. 1s.
The Sunday Scrap Book. With Several Hundred Illustrations. Paper boards, 3s. 6d.; cloth, gilt edges, 5s.
The Old Fairy Tales. With Original Illustrations. Boards, 1s.; cloth, 1s. 6d.

Albums for Children. 3s. 6d. each.

The Album for Home, School, and Play. Containing Stories by Popular Authors. Illustrated.
My Own Album of Animals. With Full-page Illustrations.
Picture Album of All Sorts. With Full-page Illustrations.
The Chit-Chat Album. Illustrated throughout.

Cassell & Company's Complete Catalogue *will be sent post free on application to*

CASSELL & COMPANY, LIMITED, *Ludgate Hill, London.*

www.ingramcontent.com/pod-product-compliance
Lightning Source LLC
Chambersburg PA
CBHW032150160426
43197CB00008B/844